12 Psychological Disorders

Learning Outcomes for Chapter 12

MODULE 37

LO 37-1 How can we distinguish normal from abnormal behavior?

LO 37-2 What are the major perspectives on psychological disorders used by mental health professionals?

LO 37-3 What are the major categories of psychological disorders?

Normal Versus Abnormal: Making the Distinction

Defining Abnormality

Perspectives on Abnormality: From Superstition to Science

Classifying Abnormal Behavior: The ABCs of *DSM*

MODULE 38

LO 38-1 What are the major psychological disorders?

The Major Psychological Disorders

Anxiety Disorders

Obsessive-Compulsive Disorder

Neuroscience in Your Life: One Step Closer to Understanding OCD

Somatoform Disorders

Dissociative Disorders

Mood Disorders

Schizophrenia

Neuroscience in Your Life: Brain Changes with Schizophrenia

Personality Disorders

Childhood Disorders

Other Disorders

MODULE 39

LO 39-1 How prevalent are psychological disorders?

LO 39-2 What indicators signal a need for the help of a mental health practitioner?

Psychological Disorders in Perspective

The Social and Cultural Context of Psychological Disorders

Applying Psychology in the 21st Century: Psychological Problems Are Increasing Among College Students

Exploring Diversity: *DSM* and Culture—and the Culture of *DSM*

Becoming an Informed Consumer of Psychology: Deciding When You Need Help

Prologue *Coping with Schizophrenia*

The first time Chris Coles heard the voice, it spoke to him after midnight. In a gentle tone, it instructed him to meet his friend at a beach cove, right then, and apologize: Chris, the voice told him, had been planning to date the friend's girlfriend. Although Coles was planning no such thing, he did as instructed, arriving at the cove at 2 a.m. It was deserted. He dismissed the incident; imagination, after all, can play tricks in the twilight between waking and dreaming. But the voices kept intruding. Coles saw visions, too. At the beach near his California home, he often saw a profusion of whales and dolphins swimming onto the beach, and a golden Buddha glowing from the bushes by the dunes. "I also had delusions of grandeur," says Coles, now 47. "I felt that I had power over things in nature, influence over the whales and dolphins and waves. I thought I could make things happen magically in the water." (Begley, 2013).

Looking **Ahead**

Chris Coles was losing his grip on reality. It turned out that he was suffering from schizophrenia, one of the more severe psychological disorders. Although drug treatments eventually stilled the voices that ran through his head, his experience raises many questions. What caused his disorder? Were genetic factors involved, or were stressors in his life primarily responsible? Were there signs that family and friends should have noticed earlier? Could his schizophrenia have been prevented? And, more generally, how do we distinguish normal from abnormal behavior, and how can Chris' behavior be categorized and classified in such a way as to pinpoint the specific nature of his problem?

We address the issues raised by Coles' case in this chapter. We begin by discussing the difference between normal and abnormal behavior, which can be surprisingly indistinct. We then turn to a consideration of the most significant kinds of psychological disorders. Finally, we'll consider ways of evaluating behavior—one's own and that of others—to determine whether seeking help from a mental health professional is warranted.

MODULE 37

Normal Versus Abnormal: Making the Distinction

Learning Outcomes

LO 37-1 How can we distinguish normal from abnormal behavior?

LO 37-2 What are the major perspectives on psychological disorders used by mental health professionals?

LO 37-3 What are the major categories of psychological disorders?

> Universally that person's acumen is esteemed very little perceptive concerning whatsoever matters are being held as most profitable by mortals with sapience endowed to be studied who is ignorant of that which the most in doctrine erudite and certainly by reason of that in them high mind's ornament deserving of veneration constantly maintain when by general consent they affirm that other circumstances being equal by no exterior splendour is the prosperity of a nation . . .

It would be easy to conclude that these words are the musings of a madman. To most people, the passage does not seem to make any sense at all. But literary scholars would disagree. Actually, this passage is from James Joyce's classic *Ulysses,* hailed as one of the major works of 20th-century literature (Joyce, 1934, p. 377).

As this example illustrates, casually examining a person's writing is insufficient to determine the degree to which that person is "normal." But even when we consider more extensive samples of a person's behavior, we will find that there may be only a fine line between behavior that is considered normal and behavior that is considered abnormal.

Defining Abnormality

Because of the difficulty in distinguishing normal from abnormal behavior, psychologists have struggled to devise a precise, scientific definition of "abnormal behavior." For instance, consider the following definitions, each of which has advantages and disadvantages:

- *Abnormality as deviation from the average.* To employ this statistically based approach, we simply observe what behaviors are rare or occur infrequently in a specific society or culture and label those deviations from the norm "abnormal."

  The difficulty with this definition is that some statistically rare behaviors clearly do not lend themselves to classification as abnormal. If most people prefer to have cornflakes for breakfast but you prefer raisin bran, this deviation hardly makes your behavior abnormal. Similarly, such a concept of abnormality would unreasonably label a person who has an unusually high IQ as abnormal simply because a high IQ is statistically rare. In short, a definition of abnormality that rests on deviation from the average is insufficient.
- *Abnormality as deviation from the ideal.* An alternative approach considers abnormality in relation to the standard toward which most people are striving—the ideal.

  This sort of definition considers behavior abnormal if it deviates enough from some kind of ideal or cultural standard. However, society has few standards on which people universally agree. (For example, we would be hard pressed to find agreement on whether the New Testament, the Koran, the Talmud, or the Book of Mormon provides the most reasonable standards.) Furthermore, standards that do arise change over time and vary across cultures. Thus, the deviation-from-the-ideal approach is also inadequate.
- *Abnormality as a sense of personal discomfort.* A more useful definition concentrates on the psychological consequences of the behavior for the individual. In this

Study Alert

Remember the different definitions of abnormality (deviation from the average, deviation from the ideal, a sense of personal discomfort, inability to function effectively, and abnormality as a legal concept).

Andrea Yates, who initially was found sane by a jury despite having drowned her five children in a bathtub, was later found innocent due to insanity.

approach, behavior is considered abnormal if it produces a sense of personal distress, anxiety, or guilt in an individual—or if it is harmful to others in some way.

Even a definition that relies on personal discomfort has drawbacks, though, because in some especially severe forms of mental disturbance, people report feeling wonderful even though their behavior seems bizarre to others. In such cases, a personal state of well-being exists, yet most people would consider the behavior abnormal. For example, most of us would think that a woman who says she is hearing uplifting messages from Martians would be displaying abnormal behavior even though she may say that the messages make her feel happy.

- *Abnormality as the inability to function effectively*. Most people are able to feed themselves, hold a job, get along with others, and in general live as productive members of society. Yet there are those who are unable to adjust to the demands of society or function effectively.

  According to this view of abnormality, people who are unable to function effectively and to adapt to the demands of society are considered abnormal. For example, an unemployed, homeless woman living on the street may be considered unable to function effectively. Therefore, her behavior can be viewed as abnormal even if she has chosen to live this way. Her inability to adapt to the requirements of society is what makes her "abnormal," according to this approach.
- *Abnormality as a legal concept*. According to the jury that first heard her case, Andrea Yates, a woman who drowned her five children in a bathtub, was sane. She was sentenced to life in prison for her act.

  Although you might question this view (and a later appeals jury overturned the conviction), the initial verdict reflected the way in which the law defines abnormal behavior. To the judicial system, the distinction between normal and abnormal behavior rests on the definition of insanity, which is a legal but not a psychological term. The definition of insanity varies from one jurisdiction to another. In some states, insanity simply means that defendants cannot understand the difference between right and wrong at the time they commit a criminal act. Other states consider whether defendants are substantially incapable of understanding the criminality of their behavior or unable to control themselves. And in some jurisdictions, pleas of insanity are not allowed at all (Frost & Bonnie, 2001; Sokolove, 2003; Ferguson & Ogloff, 2011).

Clearly, none of the previous definitions is broad enough to cover all instances of abnormal behavior. Consequently, the distinction between normal and abnormal behavior often remains ambiguous even to trained professionals. Furthermore, to a large extent, cultural expectations for "normal" behavior in a particular society influence the understanding of "abnormal behavior" (Scheff, 1998; Sanderson, 2007). Given the difficulties in precisely defining the construct, psychologists typically define **abnormal behavior** broadly as behavior that causes people to experience distress and prevents them from functioning in their daily lives (Nolen-Hoeksema, 2007). Because of the imprecision of this definition, it's best to view abnormal behavior and normal behavior as marking two ends of a continuum rather than as absolute states. Behavior should be evaluated in terms of gradations that range from fully normal functioning to extremely abnormal behavior. Behavior typically falls somewhere between those extremes.

abnormal behavior Behavior that causes people to experience distress and prevents them from functioning in their daily lives.

Perspectives on Abnormality: From Superstition to Science

Throughout much of human history, people linked abnormal behavior to superstition and witchcraft. Individuals who displayed abnormal behavior were accused of being possessed by the devil or some sort of demonic god. Authorities felt justified in "treating" abnormal behavior by attempting to drive out the source of the problem.

This typically involved whipping, immersion in hot water, starvation, or other forms of torture in which the cure was often worse than the affliction (Berrios, 1996).

Contemporary approaches take a more enlightened view. Today, six major perspectives are used to understand psychological disorders. These perspectives suggest not only different causes of abnormal behavior but different treatment approaches as well. Furthermore, some perspectives are more applicable to specific disorders than are others. Figure 1 summarizes the perspectives and the way in which they can be applied to the experience of Chris Coles, the person discussed in the chapter prologue.

Study Alert
Use Figure 1 to review the six major perspectives on abnormality and consider how they relate to the major perspectives on the field of psychology that we discussed in Chapter 1.

MEDICAL PERSPECTIVE

When people display the symptoms of tuberculosis, medical professionals can generally find tubercular bacteria in their body tissue. Similarly, the **medical perspective** suggests that when an individual displays symptoms of abnormal behavior, the fundamental cause will be found through a physical examination of the individual, which may reveal a hormonal imbalance, a chemical deficiency, or a brain injury. Indeed, when we speak of mental "illness," "symptoms" of abnormal behavior, and mental "hospitals," we are using terminology associated with the medical perspective.

medical perspective The perspective that suggests that when an individual displays symptoms of abnormal behavior, the root cause will be found in a physical examination of the individual, which may reveal a hormonal imbalance, a chemical deficiency, or a brain injury.

Because many abnormal behaviors have been linked to biological causes, the medical perspective is a reasonable approach. Yet serious criticisms have been leveled against it. For one thing, many types of abnormal behavior have no apparent biological cause. In addition, some critics have argued that the use of the term *mental illness* implies that people who display abnormal behavior have no responsibility for or control over their actions (Laing & Szasz, 2004; Szasz, 1994, 2006).

Still, recent advances in our understanding of the biological bases of behavior underscore the importance of considering physiological factors in abnormal behavior. For instance, some of the more severe forms of psychological disturbance, such as major depression and schizophrenia, are influenced by genetic factors and malfunctions in neurotransmitter signals (Iversen & Iversen, 2007; Howes & Kapur, 2009; Li et al., 2011).

PSYCHOANALYTIC PERSPECTIVE

Whereas the medical perspective suggests that biological causes are at the root of abnormal behavior, the **psychoanalytic perspective** holds that abnormal behavior stems from childhood conflicts over opposing wishes regarding sex and aggression. According to Freud, children pass through a series of stages in which sexual and aggressive impulses take different forms and produce conflicts that require resolution.

psychoanalytic perspective The perspective that suggests that abnormal behavior stems from childhood conflicts over opposing wishes regarding sex and aggression.

Perspectives on Psychological Disorders

Perspective	Description	Possible Application of Perspective to Chris' Case
Medical	Assumes that physiological causes are at the root of psychological disorders	Examine Chris for medical problems, such as brain tumor, chemical imbalance in the brain, or disease
Psychoanalytic	Argues that psychological disorders stem from childhood conflicts	Seek out information about Chris' past, considering possible childhood conflicts
Behavioral	Assumes that abnormal behaviors are learned responses	Concentrate on rewards and punishments for Chris' behavior, and identify environmental stimuli that reinforce his behavior
Cognitive	Assumes that cognitions (people's thoughts and beliefs) are central to psychological disorders	Focus on Chris' perceptions of self and his environment
Humanistic	Emphasizes people's responsibility for their own behavior and the need to self-actualize	Consider Chris' behavior in terms of his choices and efforts to reach his potential
Sociocultural	Assumes that behavior is shaped by family, society, and culture	Focus on how societal demands contributed to Chris' disorder

FIGURE 1 In considering the case of Chris Coles, discussed in the prologue, we can employ each of the different perspectives on abnormal behavior. Note, however, that because of the nature of his psychological disorder, some of the perspectives are more applicable than others.

If these childhood conflicts are not dealt with successfully, they remain unresolved in the unconscious and eventually bring about abnormal behavior during adulthood.

To uncover the roots of people's disordered behavior, the psychoanalytic perspective scrutinizes their early life history. However, because there is no conclusive way to link people's childhood experiences with the abnormal behaviors they display as adults, we can never be sure that the causes suggested by psychoanalytic theory are accurate. Moreover, psychoanalytic theory paints a picture of people as having relatively little control over their behavior because much of it is guided by unconscious impulses. In the eyes of some critics, this perspective suggests that people have little responsibility for their own behavior.

On the other hand, the contributions of psychoanalytic theory have been significant. More than any other approach to abnormal behavior, this perspective highlights the fact that people can have a rich, involved inner life and that prior experiences can have a profound effect on current psychological functioning (Elliott, 2002; Bornstein, 2003; Rangell, 2007).

BEHAVIORAL PERSPECTIVE

behavioral perspective The perspective that looks at the behavior itself as the problem.

Both the medical and psychoanalytic perspectives look at abnormal behaviors as *symptoms* of an underlying problem. In contrast, the **behavioral perspective** views the behavior itself as the problem. Using the basic principles of learning, behavioral theorists see both normal and abnormal behaviors as responses to various stimuli—responses that have been learned through past experience and are guided in the present by stimuli in the individual's environment. To explain why abnormal behavior occurs, we must analyze how an individual has learned it and observe the circumstances in which it is displayed.

The emphasis on observable behavior represents both the greatest strength and the greatest weakness of the behavioral approach to abnormal behavior. This perspective provides the most precise and objective approach for examining behavioral symptoms of specific disorders, such as attention-deficit hyperactivity disorder (ADHD), which we will discuss in a later module. At the same time, though, critics charge that the perspective ignores the rich inner world of thoughts, attitudes, and emotions that may contribute to abnormal behavior.

COGNITIVE PERSPECTIVE

The medical, psychoanalytic, and behavioral perspectives view people's behavior as the result of factors largely beyond their control. To many critics of these views, however, people's thoughts cannot be ignored.

cognitive perspective The perspective that suggests that people's thoughts and beliefs are a central component of abnormal behavior.

In response to such concerns, some psychologists employ a **cognitive perspective.** Rather than considering only external behavior, as in traditional behavioral approaches, the cognitive approach assumes that *cognitions* (people's thoughts and beliefs) are central to a person's abnormal behavior. A primary goal of treatment using the cognitive perspective is to explicitly teach new, more adaptive ways of thinking.

For instance, suppose that you develop the erroneous belief that "doing well on this exam is crucial to my entire future" whenever you take an exam. Through therapy, you might learn to hold the more realistic and less anxiety-producing thought, "my entire future is not dependent on this one exam." By changing cognitions in this way, psychologists working within a cognitive framework help people free themselves from thoughts and behaviors that are potentially maladaptive (Clark, 2004; Everly & Lating, 2007).

The cognitive perspective is not without critics. For example, it is possible that maladaptive cognitions are the symptoms or consequences of disorders rather than their cause. Furthermore, there are circumstances in which negative beliefs may not be irrational at all but simply reflect accurately the unpleasant circumstances in people's lives. Still, cognitive theorists would argue that one can find a more adaptive way of framing beliefs even in the most negative circumstances.

HUMANISTIC PERSPECTIVE

Psychologists who subscribe to the **humanistic perspective** emphasize the responsibility people have for their own behavior even when their behavior is considered abnormal. The humanistic perspective—growing out of the work of Carl Rogers and Abraham Maslow—concentrates on what is uniquely human—that is, it views people as basically rational, oriented toward a social world, and motivated to seek self-actualization (Rogers, 1995).

humanistic perspective The perspective that emphasizes the responsibility people have for their own behavior, even when such behavior is abnormal.

Humanistic approaches focus on the relationship of the individual to society; it considers the ways in which people view themselves in relation to others and see their place in the world. The humanistic perspective views people as having an awareness of life and of themselves that leads them to search for meaning and self-worth. Rather than assuming that individuals require a "cure," the humanistic perspective suggests that they can, by and large, set their own limits of what is acceptable behavior. As long as they are not hurting others and do not feel personal distress, people should be free to choose the behaviors in which they engage.

Although the humanistic perspective has been criticized for its reliance on unscientific, unverifiable information and its vague, almost philosophical formulations, it offers a distinctive view of abnormal behavior. It stresses the unique aspects of being human and provides a number of important suggestions for helping those with psychological problems.

SOCIOCULTURAL PERSPECTIVE

The **sociocultural perspective** assumes that people's behavior—both normal and abnormal—is shaped by the society and culture in which they live. According to this view, societal and cultural factors such as poverty and prejudice may be at the root of abnormal behavior. Specifically, the kinds of stresses and conflicts people experience in their daily lives can promote and maintain abnormal behavior.

sociocultural perspective The perspective that people's behavior—both normal and abnormal—is shaped by the society and culture in which they live.

This perspective is supported by research showing that some kinds of abnormal behavior are far more prevalent among certain social classes than they are in others. For instance, diagnoses of schizophrenia tend to be higher among members of lower socioeconomic groups than among members of more affluent groups. Proportionally more African-American individuals are hospitalized involuntarily for psychological disorders than are whites. Furthermore, poor economic times seem to be linked to general declines in psychological functioning, and social problems such as homelessness are associated with psychological disorders (Nasir & Hand, 2006; Greenberg & Rosenheck, 2008; Padgett, Stanhope, & Henwood, 2011).

On the other hand, alternative explanations abound for the association between abnormal behavior and social factors. For example, people from lower socioeconomic levels may be less likely than those from higher levels to seek help, gradually reaching a point where their symptoms become severe and warrant a serious diagnosis. Furthermore, sociocultural explanations provide relatively little specific guidance for the treatment of individuals showing mental disturbance because the focus is on broader societal factors (Paniagua, 2000).

Classifying Abnormal Behavior: The ABCs of *DSM*

Crazy. Whacked. Mental. Loony. Insane. Neurotic. Psycho. Strange. Demented. Odd. Possessed.

Society has long placed labels on people who display abnormal behavior. Unfortunately, most of the time these labels have reflected intolerance and have been used with little thought as to what each label signifies.

Providing appropriate and specific names and classifications for abnormal behavior has presented a major challenge to psychologists. It is not hard to understand why, given the difficulties discussed earlier in simply distinguishing normal from abnormal behavior. Yet psychologists and other careproviders need to classify abnormal behavior in order to diagnose it and ultimately treat it.

DSM-5: DETERMINING DIAGNOSTIC DISTINCTIONS

Over the years, mental health professionals have developed many different classification systems that vary in terms of their utility and the degree to which they have been accepted. However, one standard system, devised by the American Psychiatric Association, has emerged in the United States. Most professionals today use this classification system, known as the ***Diagnostic and Statistical Manual of Mental Disorders,* Fifth Edition, *(DSM-5)*** to diagnose and classify abnormal behavior (American Psychiatric Association, 2013).

Diagnostic and Statistical Manual of Mental Disorders, **Fifth Edition,** *(DSM-5)* A system, devised by the American Psychiatric Association, used by most professionals to diagnose and classify abnormal behavior.

The *DSM-5,* most recently revised in 2013, attempts to provide comprehensive and relatively precise definitions for more than 200 disorders. By following the criteria presented in the *DSM-5* classification system, diagnosticians use clients' reported symptoms to identify the specific problem an individual is experiencing. (Figure 2 provides a brief outline of the major diagnostic categories; American Psychiatric Association, 2013).

The manual takes an *atheoretical* approach to identifying psychological disorders, though some practitioners have argued that this diagnostic approach is too heavily based on a medical model. The authors of the newest update of DSM suggest that the manual should be viewed as the "DSM-5.0." The "5.0" name emphasizes that the *DSM-5* is a work in progress, subject to revision based on users' feedback. (The next revision will be called DSM-5.1.)

Among the major changes to *DSM-5* are the following (Kupfer, Kuhl, & Regier, 2013; Wakefield, 2013):

- **A lifespan development focus.** Disorders have been rearranged in terms of what age they are likely to first appear. In addition, the *DSM-5* is more specific about how the same disorder may change over the course of a person's lifetime.
- **Childhood and late-life conditions have been renamed.** Along with removing the outdated term "mental retardation" in favor of *intellectual disability,* the *DSM-5* renames childhood conditions as *neurodevelopmental disorders,* and "dementia and amnestic disorders" as *neurocognitive disorders.*
- **Autism disorder has been reclassified.** Different forms of autism are now grouped together and called *Autism Spectrum Disorder (ASD),* which focuses on the degree of severity of autism.
- **Sexually based disorders have been reconceptualized and renamed.** "Gender identity disorder" has been reclassified as *gender dysphoria.* This distinction makes it clear that having a gender identity that is in conflict with one's biological sex does not imply a psychological disorder. Additionally, "paraphilia" has been renamed *paraphilic disorders,* emphasizing the presence of some atypical sexual interests that do not necessarily indicate a psychological disorder.
- **Criteria for some disorders have been made less restrictive.** In particular, the conditions that need to be met for an adult attention-deficit hyperactivity disorder (ADHD) diagnosis are broader—meaning that more people are likely to be classified with adult ADHD. Additionally, bereaved clients are no longer diagnosed with depression if symptoms arose within a few months of the death of a loved one.
- **The "five axes model" is eliminated.** In the previous version of DSM, disorders were categorized along one of five axes (Axis I, Clinical Disorders; Axis II, Personality Disorders and Mental Retardation; Axis III, General Medical Conditions; Axis IV, Psychosocial and Environmental Problems; and Axis V, Global Assessment of Functioning). These axes have been eliminated from the new version of *DSM-5.*

Categories of Disorders	Examples
Anxiety (problems in which anxiety impedes daily functioning)	Generalized anxiety disorder, panic disorder, phobic disorder, posttraumatic stress disorder
Somatoform (psychological difficulties displayed through physical problems)	Hypochondriasis, conversion disorder
Dissociative (the splitting apart of crucial parts of personality that are usually integrated)	Dissociative identity disorder (multiple personality), dissociative amnesia, dissociative fugue
Mood (emotions of depression or euphoria that are so strong they intrude on everyday living)	Major depression, bipolar disorder
Schizophrenia and psychotic disorders (declines in functioning, thought and language disturbances, perception disorders, emotional disturbances, and withdrawal from others)	Delusional disorder
Personality (problems that create little personal distress but that lead to an inability to function as a normal member of society)	Antisocial (sociopathic) personality disorder, narcissistic personality disorder
Sexual (problems related to sexual arousal from unusual objects or problems related to functioning)	Paraphilic disorders, sexual dysfunction
Substance-related (problems related to drug dependence and abuse)	Alcohol, cocaine, hallucinogens, marijuana
Dementia, amnesia, and other cognitive disorders	Alzheimer's

FIGURE 2 This list of disorders represents the major categories from the *DSM-5.* It is only a partial list of the scores of disorders included in the manual.

In many other respects, the *DSM* remains unchanged in the newest revision. Like its predecessors, *DSM-5* is primarily descriptive and avoids suggesting an underlying cause for an individual's behavior and problems. For instance, the term *neurotic*—a label that is commonly used by people in their everyday descriptions of abnormal behavior—is not listed as a *DSM* category. Because the term *neurosis* refers to problems associated with a specific cause based in Freud's theory of personality, it is not included in *DSM-5*.

DSM-5 has the advantage, then, of providing a descriptive system that does not specify the cause of or reason for a problem. Rather, it paints a picture of the behavior that is being displayed. Why should this approach be important? For one thing, it allows communication between mental health professionals of diverse backgrounds and theoretical approaches. In addition, precise classification enables researchers to explore the causes of a problem. Without reliable descriptions of abnormal behavior, researchers would be hard pressed to find ways to investigate the disorder. Finally, *DSM-5* provides a kind of conceptual shorthand through which professionals can describe the behaviors that tend to occur together in an individual (First, Frances, & Pincus, 2002; Gordon & Heimberg, 2011).

CONNING THE CLASSIFIERS: THE SHORTCOMINGS OF *DSM*

When clinical psychologist David Rosenhan and eight colleagues sought admission to separate mental hospitals across the United States in the 1970s, each stated that he or she was hearing voices—"unclear voices" that said "empty," "hollow," and "thud"—and each was immediately admitted to the hospital. However, the truth was that they actually were conducting a study, and none of them was really hearing voices. Aside from these misrepresentations, *everything* else they did and said represented their true behavior, including the responses they gave during extensive admission interviews and their answers to the battery of tests they were asked to complete. In fact, as soon as they were admitted, they said they no longer heard any voices. In short, each of the pseudo-patients acted in a "normal" way (Rosenhan, 1973).

We might assume that Rosenhan and his colleagues would have been quickly discovered as the impostors they were, but this was not the case. Instead, each of them was diagnosed as severely abnormal on the basis of observed behavior. Mental health professionals labeled most as suffering from schizophrenia and kept them in the hospital 3–52 days, with the average stay of 19 days. Even when they were discharged, most of the "patients" left with the label *schizophrenia—in remission,* implying that the abnormal behavior had only temporarily subsided and could recur at any time. Most disturbing, no one on the hospital staff identified any of the pseudo-patients as impostors—although some of the actual patients figured out the ruse.

The results of Rosenhan's classic study illustrate that placing labels on individuals powerfully influences the way mental health workers perceive and interpret their actions. It also points out that determining who is psychologically disordered is not always a clear-cut or accurate process.

Gender dysphoria (in which one's gender identity is in conflict with one's biological sex) provides a modern illustration of the dilemma between the pros of a formal diagnosis and the cons of patient labeling. For example, most medical insurance providers *require* a formal, specific diagnosis in order to receive healthcare coverage for procedures such as a sex change operation. Many individuals who experience a conflict between their gender identity and their biological sex object theoretically to the idea that their desire to be the other sex should be labeled a "disorder." Yet without a formal diagnosis, those same individuals may be forced to pay out-of-pocket for what is an expensive medical procedure. This diagnosis-based system of insurance coverage often creates a Catch-22 for mental health care professionals: They must decide between potentially stigmatizing their clients by providing a formal diagnosis, implying some type of disorder, or leaving patients undiagnosed and potentially without the financial support necessary to receive important procedures that will significantly improve their client's quality of life (Kamens, 2011; Kleinplatz, Moser, & Lev, 2013).

Critics of the DSM argue that labeling an individual as abnormal provides a dehumanizing, lifelong stigma. (Think, for example, of political contenders whose candidacies have been terminated by the disclosure that they received treatment for severe psychological disorders.) Furthermore, after an initial diagnosis has been made, mental health professionals, who may concentrate on the initial diagnostic category, could overlook other diagnostic possibilities (McNally, 2011; Szasz, 2011; Frances, 2013).

Although the *DSM-5* was developed to provide more accurate and consistent diagnoses of psychological disorders, it isn't always successful. For instance, critics charge that it relies too much on the medical perspective. Because it was drawn up by psychiatrists—who are physicians—some condemn it for viewing psychological disorders primarily in terms of the symptoms of an underlying physiological disorder. Moreover, critics suggest that *DSM-5* compartmentalizes people into inflexible, all-or-none categories rather than considering the degree to which a person displays psychologically disordered behavior (Samuel & Widiger, 2006; Frances, 2013).

Study Alert
It is important to understand the advantages and weaknesses of the *DSM* classification system.

Still, despite the drawbacks inherent in any labeling system, the *DSM-5* has had an important influence on the way in which mental health professionals view psychological disorders. It has increased both the reliability and the validity of diagnostic categorization. In addition, it offers a logical way to organize examination of the major types of mental disturbance.

RECAP/EVALUATE/RETHINK

RECAP

LO 37-1 How can we distinguish normal from abnormal behavior?

- Definitions of abnormality include deviation from the average, deviation from the ideal, a sense of personal discomfort, the inability to function effectively, and legal conceptions. (pp. 453, 454)
- Although no single definition is adequate, abnormal behavior can be considered to be behavior that causes people to experience distress and prevents them from functioning in their daily lives. Most psychologists believe that abnormal and normal behavior should be considered in terms of a continuum. (p. 454)

LO 37-2 What are the major perspectives on psychological disorders used by mental health professionals?

- The medical perspective views abnormality as a symptom of an underlying disease. (p. 455)
- Psychoanalytic perspectives suggest that abnormal behavior stems from childhood conflicts in the unconscious. (p. 455)
- Behavioral approaches view abnormal behavior not as a symptom of an underlying problem but as the problem itself. (p. 456)
- The cognitive approach suggests that abnormal behavior is the result of faulty cognitions (thoughts and beliefs). In this view, abnormal behavior can be remedied by changing one's flawed thoughts and beliefs. (p. 456)
- Humanistic approaches emphasize the responsibility people have for their own behavior even when such behavior is seen as abnormal. (p. 457)
- Sociocultural approaches view abnormal behavior in terms of difficulties arising from family and other social relationships. (p. 457)

LO 37-3 What are the major categories of psychological disorders?

- The most widely used system for classifying psychological disorders is *DSM-5—Diagnostic and Statistical Manual of Mental Disorders,* Fifth Edition. (p. 458)

EVALUATE

1. One problem in defining abnormal behavior is that
   - **a.** Statistically rare behavior may not be abnormal.
   - **b.** Not all abnormalities are accompanied by feelings of discomfort.
   - **c.** Cultural standards are too general to use as a measuring tool.
   - **d.** All of the above.
2. If abnormality is defined as behavior that causes personal discomfort or harms others, which of the following people is most likely to need treatment?
   - **a.** An executive is afraid to accept a promotion because it would require moving from his ground-floor office to the top floor of a tall office building.
   - **b.** A woman decides to quit her job and chooses to live on the street in order to live a "simpler life."
   - **c.** A man believes that friendly spacemen visit his house every Thursday.
   - **d.** A photographer lives with 19 cats in a small apartment lovingly caring for them.
3. Virginia's mother thinks that her daughter's behavior is clearly abnormal because, despite being offered admission to medical school, Virginia decides to become a waitress. What approach is Virginia's mother using to define abnormal behavior?
4. Which of the following is a strong argument against the medical perspective on abnormality?
   - **a.** Physiological abnormalities are almost always impossible to identify.
   - **b.** There is no conclusive way to link past experience and behavior.
   - **c.** The medical perspective rests too heavily on the effects of nutrition.
   - **d.** Assigning behavior to a physical problem takes responsibility away from the individual for changing his or her behavior.
5. Cheryl is painfully shy. According to the behavioral perspective, the best way to deal with her "abnormal" behavior is to
   - **a.** Treat the underlying physical problem.
   - **b.** Use the principles of learning theory to modify her shy behavior.
   - **c.** Express a great deal of caring.
   - **d.** Uncover her negative past experiences through hypnosis.

RETHINK

1. Do you agree or disagree that *DSM* should be updated every several years? Why? What makes abnormal behavior so variable?
2. *From the perspective of an employer:* Imagine that a well-paid employee was arrested for shoplifting a sweater that costs $15. What sort of explanation for this behavior would the proponents of *each* perspective on abnormality provide: the medical perspective, the psychoanalytic perspective, the behavioral perspective, the cognitive perspective, the humanistic perspective, and the sociocultural perspective? Based on the potential causes of the shoplifting, would you fire the employee? Why or why not?

Answers to Evaluate Questions

1. d; 2. a; 3. deviation from the ideal; 4. d; 5. b

KEY TERMS

abnormal behavior p. 453
medical perspective p. 455
psychoanalytic perspective p. 455
behavioral perspective p. 456
cognitive perspective p. 456
humanistic perspective p. 457
sociocultural perspective p. 457
Diagnostic and Statistical Manual of Mental Disorders*, Fifth Edition, *(DSM-5) p. 458

MODULE 38

The Major Psychological Disorders

> Sally experienced her first panic attack out of the blue, 3 weeks after completing her senior year in college. She had just finished a job interview and was meeting some friends for dinner. In the restaurant, she began to feel dizzy. Within a few seconds, her heart was pounding, and she was feeling breathless, as though she might pass out. Her friends noticed that she did not look well and offered to drive her home. Sally suggested they stop at the hospital emergency room instead. Although she felt better by the time they arrived at the hospital, and tests indicated nothing wrong, Sally experienced a similar episode a week later while at a movie. . . .
>
> Her attacks became more and more frequent. Before long, she was having several attacks per week. In addition, she constantly worried about having attacks. She began to avoid exercise and other activities that produced physical sensations. She also noticed the attacks were worse when she was alone. She began to avoid driving, shopping in large stores, and eating in all restaurants. Some weeks she avoided leaving the house completely. (Antony, Brown, & Barlow, 1992, p. 79)

Learning Outcome

LO 38-1 What are the major psychological disorders?

Sally suffered from panic disorder, one of the specific psychological disorders we'll consider in this module. Keep in mind that although we'll be discussing these disorders objectively, each represents a very human set of difficulties that influence and in some cases considerably disrupt people's lives.

Anxiety Disorders

All of us at one time or another experience *anxiety,* a feeling of apprehension or tension, in reaction to stressful situations. There is nothing "wrong" with such anxiety. It is a normal reaction to stress that often helps rather than hinders our daily functioning. Without some anxiety, for instance, most of us probably would not have much motivation to study hard, undergo physical exams, or spend long hours at our jobs.

But some people experience anxiety in situations in which there is no apparent reason or cause for such distress. **Anxiety disorders** occur when anxiety arises without external justification and begins to affect people's daily functioning. We'll discuss three major types of anxiety disorders: phobic disorder, panic disorder, and generalized anxiety disorder.

anxiety disorder The occurrence of anxiety without an obvious external cause that affects daily functioning.

PHOBIC DISORDER

> It's not easy moving through the world when you're terrified of electricity. "Donna," 45, a writer, knows that better than most. Get her in the vicinity of an appliance or a light switch or—all but unthinkable—a thunderstorm, and she is overcome by a terror so blinding she can think of nothing but fleeing. That, of course, is not always possible, so over time, Donna has come up with other answers. When she opens the refrigerator door, rubber-sole shoes are a must. If a light bulb blows, she will tolerate the dark until someone else changes it for her. Clothes shopping is done only when necessary, lest static on garments send her running from the store. And swimming at night is absolutely out of the question, lest underwater lights electrocute her. (Kluger, 2001, p. 51)

Phobic Disorder	Description	Example
Agoraphobia	Fear of places, such as unfamiliar or crowded spaces, where help might not be available in case of emergency	Person becomes housebound because any place other than the person's home arouses extreme anxiety symptoms. 
Specific phobias	Fear of specific objects, places, or situations	
Animal type	Specific animals or insects 	Person has extreme fear of dogs, cats, or spiders.
Natural environment type	Events or situations in the natural environment	Person has extreme fear of storms, heights, or water.
Situational type	Public transportation, tunnels, bridges, elevators, flying, driving	Person becomes extremely claustrophobic in elevators. 
Blood injection-injury type	Blood, injury, injections 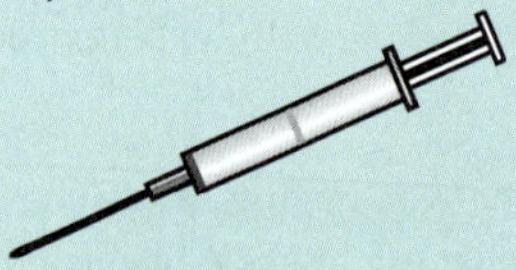	Person panics when viewing a child's scraped knee.
Social phobia	Fear of being judged or embarrassed by others	Person avoids all social situations and becomes a recluse for fear of encountering others' judgment.

FIGURE 1 Phobic disorders differ from generalized anxiety and panic disorders because a specific stimulus can be identified. Listed here are a number of types of phobias and their triggers. (Source: Adapted from Nolen-Hoeksema, 2007.)

phobias Intense, irrational fears of specific objects or situations.

Donna suffers from a **phobia,** an intense, irrational fear of a specific object or situation. For example, claustrophobia is a fear of enclosed places, acrophobia is a fear of high places, xenophobia is a fear of strangers, social phobia is the fear of being judged or embarrassed by others, and—as in Donna's case—electrophobia is a fear of electricity.

The objective danger posed by an anxiety-producing stimulus (which can be just about anything, as you can see in Figure 1) is typically small or nonexistent. However, to someone suffering from the phobia, the danger is great, and a full-blown panic attack may follow exposure to the stimulus. Phobic disorders differ from generalized anxiety disorders and panic disorders in that there is a specific, identifiable stimulus that sets off the anxiety reaction.

Phobias may have only a minor impact on people's lives if those who suffer from them can avoid the stimuli that trigger fear. For example, a fear of heights may have little impact on people's everyday lives (although it may prevent them from living in a high floor in an apartment)—unless they are firefighters or window-washers. On the other hand, a *social phobia,* or a fear of strangers, presents a more serious problem. In one extreme case, a Washington woman left her home just three times in 30 years—once to visit her family, once for an operation, and once to purchase ice cream for a dying companion (Kimbrel, 2007; Wong, Sarver, & Beidel, 2011).

PANIC DISORDER

panic disorder Anxiety disorder that takes the form of panic attacks lasting from a few seconds to several hours.

In another type of anxiety disorder, **panic disorder,** *panic attacks* occur that last from a few seconds to several hours. Unlike phobias, which are stimulated by specific objects or situations, panic disorders do not have any identifiable stimuli. Instead, during an attack such as those Sally experienced in the case described earlier, anxiety suddenly—and often without warning—rises to a peak, and an individual feels a sense of impending, unavoidable doom. Although the physical symptoms differ from person to person, they may include heart palpitations, shortness of breath, unusual amounts of sweating, faintness and dizziness, gastric sensations, and sometimes a sense of imminent death. After such an attack, it is no wonder that people tend to feel exhausted (Rachman & deSilva, 2004; Laederach-Hofmann & Messerli-Buergy, 2007; Montgomery, 2011).

Panic attacks seemingly come out of nowhere and are unconnected to any specific stimulus. Because they don't know what triggers their feelings of panic, victims of panic attacks may become fearful of going places. In fact, some people with panic disorder develop a complication called *agoraphobia*, the fear of being in a situation in which escape is difficult and in which help for a possible panic attack would not be available. In extreme cases, people with agoraphobia never leave their homes (Herrán, Carrera, & Sierra-Biddle, 2006; Wittchen et al., 2008; McTeague et al., 2011).

In addition to the physical symptoms, panic disorder affects how the brain processes information. For instance, people with panic disorder have reduced reactions in the anterior cingulate cortex to stimuli (such as viewing a fearful face) that normally produce a strong reaction in those without the disorder. It may be that recurring high levels of emotional arousal that patients with panic disorder experience desensitizes them to emotional stimuli (Pillay et al., 2006; Pillay et al., 2007).

Acrophobia, the fear of heights, is not an uncommon phobia. What sort of behavior-modification approaches might be used to deal with acrophobia?

GENERALIZED ANXIETY DISORDER

People with **generalized anxiety disorder** experience long-term, persistent anxiety and uncontrollable worry. Sometimes their concerns are about identifiable issues involving family, money, work, or health. In other cases, though, people with the disorder feel that something dreadful is about to happen but can't identify the reason and thus experience "free-floating" anxiety.

generalized anxiety disorder The experience of long-term, persistent anxiety and worry.

Because of persistent anxiety, people with generalized anxiety disorder cannot concentrate or set their worry and fears aside; their lives become centered on their worry. Furthermore, their anxiety is often accompanied by physiological symptoms such as muscle tension, headaches, dizziness, heart palpitations, or insomnia (Starcevic et al., 2007). Figure 2 on page 466 shows the most common symptoms of generalized anxiety disorder.

Obsessive-Compulsive Disorder

In **obsessive-compulsive disorder (OCD),** people are plagued by unwanted thoughts, called obsessions, or feel that they must carry out behaviors, termed compulsions, which they feel driven to perform.

obsessive-compulsive disorder (OCD) A disorder characterized by obsessions or compulsions.

An **obsession** is a persistent, unwanted thought or idea that keeps recurring. For example, a student may be unable to stop thinking that she has neglected to put her name on a test and may think about it constantly for the 2 weeks it takes to get the paper back. A man may go on vacation and wonder the whole time whether he locked his house. A woman may hear the same tune running through her head over and over. In each case, the thought or idea is unwanted and difficult to put out of mind. Of course, many people suffer from mild obsessions from time to time, but usually such thoughts persist only for a short period. For people with serious obsessions, however, the thoughts persist for days or months and may consist of bizarre, troubling images (Lee et al., 2005; Rassin & Muris, 2007; Wenzel, 2011).

obsession A persistent, unwanted thought or idea that keeps recurring.

As part of an obsessive-compulsive disorder, people may also experience **compulsions,** irresistible urges to repeatedly carry out some act that seems strange and unreasonable even to them. Whatever the compulsive behavior is, people experience extreme

compulsion An irresistible urge to repeatedly carry out some act that seems strange and unreasonable.

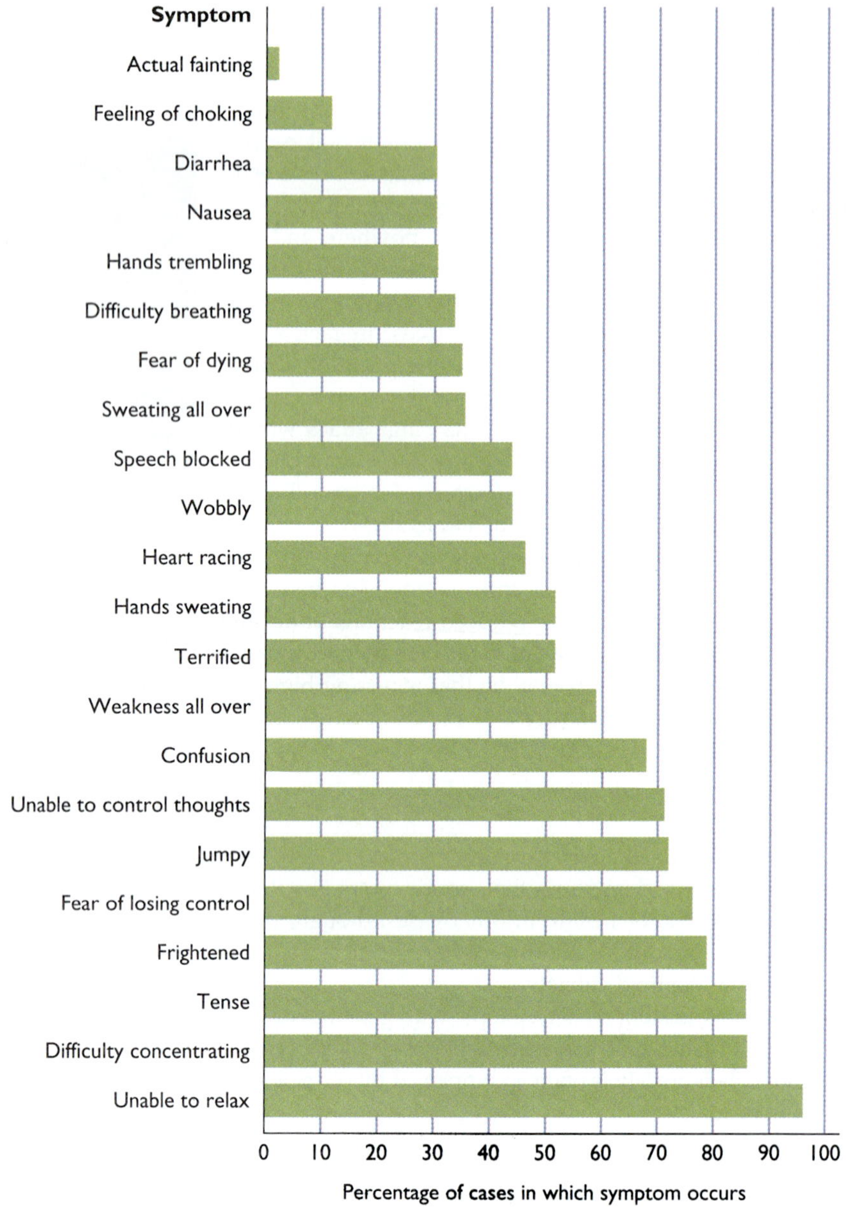

FIGURE 2 Frequency of symptoms in cases of generalized anxiety disorder. (Source: Adapted from Beck & Emery, 1985, pp. 87–88.)

anxiety if they cannot carry it out even if it is something they want to stop. The acts may be relatively trivial, such as repeatedly checking the stove to make sure all the burners are turned off, or more unusual, such as washing one's hands so much that they bleed (Frost & Steketee, 2002; Clark, 2007; Moretz & McKay, 2009).

For example, consider this passage from the autobiography of a person with obsessive-compulsive disorder:

> I thought my parents would die if I didn't do everything in exactly the right way. When I took my glasses off at night I'd have to place them on the dresser at a particular angle. Sometimes I'd turn on the light and get out of bed seven times until I felt comfortable with the angle. If the angle wasn't right, I felt that my parents would die. The feeling ate up my insides.
>
> If I didn't grab the molding on the wall just the right way as I entered or exited my room; if I didn't hang a shirt in the closet perfectly; if I didn't read a paragraph a certain way; if my hands and nails weren't perfectly clean, I thought my incorrect behavior would kill my parents. (Summers, 2000, p. 42)

Although carrying out compulsive rituals may lead to some immediate reduction of anxiety, in the long run the anxiety returns. In fact, people with severe cases lead lives filled with unrelenting tension (Goodman, Rudorfer, & Maser, 2000; Penzel, 2000; Dittrich, Johansen, & Fineberg, 2011).

PsychTech

Although some people seem to use the Internet compulsively, psychologists have yet to agree on whether it represents a true psychological disorder.

THE CAUSES OF ANXIETY DISORDERS AND OBSESSIVE-COMPULSIVE DISORDER

We've considered several of the major types of anxiety disorders and obsessive-compulsive disorder, but there are many other related disorders. For instance, *post-traumatic stress disorder* (in which a person re-experiences a stressful event in vivid flashbacks or dreams and which we discussed when we considered stress) is classified as an anxiety disorder.

The variety of anxiety disorders means that no single explanation fits all cases. Genetic factors clearly are part of the picture. For example, if one member of a pair of identical twins has panic disorder, there is a 30% chance that the other twin will have it also. Furthermore, a person's characteristic level of anxiety is related to a specific gene involved in the production of the neurotransmitter serotonin. This is consistent with findings indicating that certain chemical deficiencies in the brain appear to produce some kinds of anxiety disorder (Holmes et al., 2003; Beidel & Turner, 2007; Chamberlain et al., 2008).

Some researchers believe that an overactive autonomic nervous system may be at the root of panic attacks. Specifically, they suggest that poor regulation of the brain's locus ceruleus may lead to panic attacks, which cause the limbic system to become overstimulated. In turn, the overstimulated limbic system produces chronic anxiety, which ultimately leads the locus ceruleus to generate still more panic attacks (Pine et al., 2000; Balaban, 2002; Davies et al., 2008).

There are also biological causes at work in OCD. For example, researchers have found differences in the brains of those with the disorder compared to those without it (see Figure 3 *Neuroscience in Your Life;* Christian et al., 2008).

"Spin your partner round and round, then spin your partner round again, spin her round six more times, now touch the light switch near the door."

Neuroscience in Your Life: One Step Closer to Understanding OCD

FIGURE 3 People with obsessive-compulsive disorder (OCD) have structural differences in their brains. These images show increased levels of gray matter (i.e., more connections or more neurons) in the thalamus (a) and in the left frontal cortex (b) in people with OCD as compared to people without it. These findings help us to understand the potential causes of OCD and may lead to the development of better treatments for the disorder. (Source: Christian et al., 2008, Figure 1.)

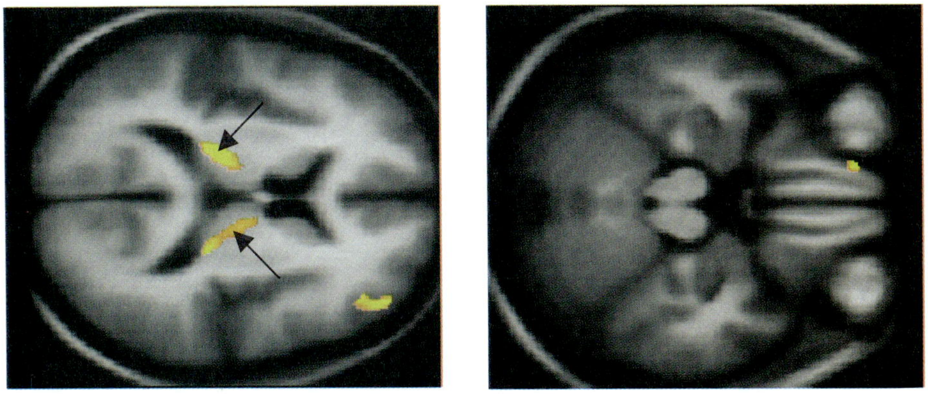

(a) (b)

Psychologists who employ the behavioral perspective have taken a different approach that emphasizes environmental factors. They consider anxiety to be a learned response to stress. For instance, suppose a dog bites a young girl. When the girl next sees a dog, she is frightened and runs away—a behavior that relieves her anxiety and thereby reinforces her avoidance behavior. After repeated encounters with dogs in which she is reinforced for her avoidance behavior, she may develop a full-fledged phobia regarding dogs.

Finally, the cognitive perspective suggests that anxiety disorders grow out of inappropriate and inaccurate thoughts and beliefs about circumstances in a person's world. For example, people with anxiety disorders may view a friendly puppy as a ferocious and savage pit bull, or they may see an air disaster looming every moment they are in the vicinity of an airplane. According to the cognitive perspective, people's maladaptive thoughts about the world are at the root of an anxiety disorder (Frost & Steketee, 2002; Wang & Clark, 2002; Ouimet, Gawronski, & Dozois, 2009).

Somatoform Disorders

somatoform disorders Psychological difficulties that take on a physical (somatic) form, but for which there is no medical cause.

hypochondriasis A disorder in which people have a constant fear of illness and a preoccupation with their health.

conversion disorder A major somatoform disorder that involves an actual physical disturbance, such as the inability to use a sensory organ or the complete or partial inability to move an arm or leg.

Somatoform disorders are psychological difficulties that take on a physical (somatic) form but for which there is no medical cause. Even though an individual with a somatoform disorder reports physical symptoms, no biological cause exists, or if there is a medical problem, the person's reaction is greatly exaggerated.

One type of somatoform disorder is **hypochondriasis** in which people have a constant fear of illness and a preoccupation with their health. These individuals believe that everyday aches and pains are symptoms of a dread disease. The "symptoms" are not faked; rather, they are misinterpreted as evidence of some serious illness—often in the face of inarguable medical evidence to the contrary (Abramowitz, Olatunji, & Deacon, 2007; Olatunji, 2008; Weck et al., 2011).

Another somatoform disorder is conversion disorder. Unlike hypochondriasis, in which there is no physical problem, **conversion disorders** involve an actual physical disturbance, such as the inability to see or hear or to move an arm or leg. The *cause* of such a physical disturbance is purely psychological; there is no biological reason for the problem. Some of Freud's classic cases involved conversion disorders. For instance, one of Freud's patients suddenly became unable to use her arm without any apparent physiological cause. Later, just as abruptly, the problem disappeared.

Conversion disorders often begin suddenly. Previously normal people wake up one day blind or deaf, or they experience numbness that is restricted to a certain part of the body. A hand, for example, may become entirely numb, while an area above the wrist, controlled by the same nerves, remains sensitive to touch—something that is physiologically implausible. Mental health professionals refer to such a condition as "glove anesthesia" because the numb area is the part of the hand covered by a glove and not a region related to pathways of the nervous system (see Figure 4).

Surprisingly, people who experience conversion disorders frequently remain unconcerned about symptoms that most of us would expect to be highly anxiety producing. For instance, a person in good health who wakes up blind may react in a bland, matter-of-fact way. Considering how most of us would feel if we woke up unable to see, this unemotional reaction (called *la belle indifference,* a French phrase meaning "a beautiful indifference") hardly seems appropriate (Brasic, 2002).

Dissociative Disorders

dissociative disorders Psychological dysfunctions characterized by the separation of different facets of a person's personality that are normally integrated.

The classic movie *The Three Faces of Eve* (about a woman with three wildly different personalities) and the book *Sybil* (about a girl who allegedly had 16 personalities) represent a highly dramatic, rare, and controversial class of disorders: dissociative disorders. **Dissociative disorders** are characterized by the separation (or dissociation)

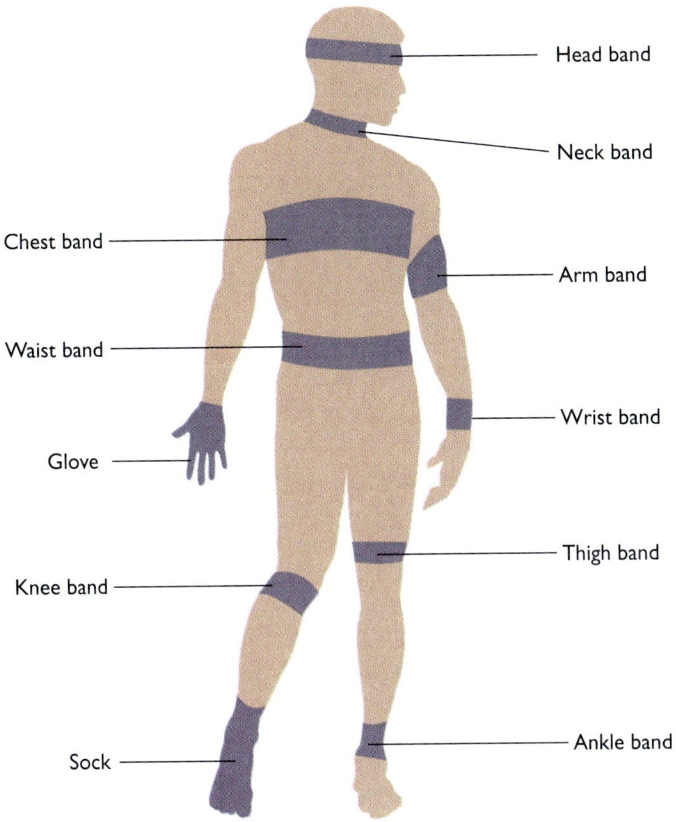

FIGURE 4 Conversion disorders sometimes produce numbness in specific and isolated areas of the body (indicated by the shaded areas in the figure). For instance, in glove anesthesia, the area of the body covered by a glove feels numb. However, the condition is biologically implausible because of the nerves involved, which suggests that the problem results from a psychological disorder rather than from actual nerve damage.

of different facets of a person's personality that are normally integrated and work together. By dissociating key parts of who they are, people are able to keep disturbing memories or perceptions from reaching conscious awareness and thereby reduce their anxiety (Maldonado & Spiegel, 2003; Houghtalen & Talbot, 2007).

Several dissociative disorders exist, although all of them are rare. A person with a **dissociative identity disorder (DID)** (once called *multiple personality disorder*) displays characteristics of two or more distinct personalities, identities, or personality fragments. Individual personalities often have a unique set of likes and dislikes and their own reactions to situations. Some people with multiple personalities even carry several pairs of glasses because their vision changes with each personality. Moreover, each individual personality can be well adjusted when considered on its own (Ellason & Ross, 2004; Stickley & Nickeas, 2006; Howell, 2011).

dissociative identity disorder (DID) A disorder in which a person displays characteristics of two or more distinct personalities.

The diagnosis of dissociative identity disorder is controversial. It was rarely diagnosed before 1980, when it was added as a category in the third edition of *DSM* for the first time. At that point, the number of cases increased significantly. Some clinicians suggest the increase was due to more precise identification of the disorder, while others suggest the increase was due to an overreadiness to use the classification. In addition, widespread publicity about cases of DID may have influenced patients to report symptoms of more common personality disorders in ways that made it more likely they would receive a diagnosis of DID. There are also significant cross-cultural differences in the incidence of DID (Kihlstrom, 2005a; Xiao et al., 2006).

Dissociative amnesia is another dissociative disorder in which a significant, selective memory loss occurs. Dissociative amnesia is unlike simple amnesia, which involves an actual loss of information from memory and typically results from a physiological

dissociative amnesia A disorder in which a significant, selective memory loss occurs.

cause. In contrast, in cases of dissociative amnesia, the "forgotten" material is still present in memory—it simply cannot be recalled. The term *repressed memories* is sometimes used to describe the lost memories of people with dissociative amnesia.

In the most severe form of dissociative amnesia, individuals cannot recall their names, are unable to recognize parents and other relatives, and do not know their addresses. In other respects, though, they may appear quite normal. Apart from an inability to remember certain facts about themselves, they may be able to recall skills and abilities that they developed earlier. For instance, even though a chef may not remember where he grew up and received training, he may still be able to prepare gourmet meals.

In some cases of dissociative amnesia, the memory loss is profound. For example, in one dramatic case, Raymond Power Jr., an attorney, husband, father of two, and Boy Scout leader, left home to go to work one morning. Two days later he was homeless, living a new life a thousand miles away, and had no memory of who he was or how he got there. He was found 6 months later but still had no recollection of his previous life, including any knowledge of his wife of 30 years or even that he had children (Foderaro, 2006).

dissociative fugue A form of amnesia in which the individual leaves home and sometimes assumes a new identity.

A more unusual form of amnesia is a condition known as **dissociative fugue.** In this state, people take sudden, impulsive trips and sometimes assume a new identity. After a period of time—days, months, or sometimes even years—they suddenly realize that they are in a strange place and completely forget the time they have spent wandering. Their last memories are those from the time just before they entered the fugue state (Hennig-Fast et al., 2008).

The common thread among dissociative disorders is that they allow people to escape from some anxiety-producing situation. Either the person produces a new personality to deal with stress, or the individual forgets or leaves behind the situation that caused the stress as he or she journeys to some new—and perhaps less anxiety-ridden—environment (Putnam, 2000; R. J. Brown, 2006).

Mood Disorders

> From the time I woke up in the morning until the time I went to bed at night, I was unbearably miserable and seemingly incapable of any kind of joy or enthusiasm. Everything—every thought, word, movement—was an effort. Everything that once was sparkling now was flat. I seemed to myself to be dull, boring, inadequate, thick brained, unlit, unresponsive, chill skinned, bloodless, and sparrow drab. I doubted, completely, my ability to do anything well. It seemed as though my mind had slowed down and burned out to the point of being virtually useless. (Jamison, 1995, p. 110)

We all experience mood swings. Sometimes we are happy, perhaps even euphoric; at other times we feel upset, saddened, or depressed. Such changes in mood are a normal part of everyday life. In some people, however, moods are so pronounced and lingering—like the feelings described above by writer (and psychiatrist) Kay Jamison—that they interfere with the ability to function effectively. In extreme cases, a mood may become life threatening; in other cases, it may cause the person to lose touch with reality. Situations such as these represent **mood disorders,** disturbances in emotional experience that are strong enough to intrude on everyday living.

mood disorder A disturbance in emotional experience that is strong enough to intrude on everyday living.

MAJOR DEPRESSION

President Abraham Lincoln. Queen Victoria. Newscaster Mike Wallace.

major depression A severe form of depression that interferes with concentration, decision making, and sociability.

The common link among these people? Each suffered from periodic attacks of **major depression,** a severe form of depression that interferes with concentration, decision making, and sociability. Major depression is one of the more common forms of mood disorders. Some 15 million people in the United States suffer from major depression, and at any one time, 6–10% of the U.S. population is clinically depressed. Almost one in five people in the United States experiences major depression at some point in life, and 15% of college students have received a diagnosis of depression. The cost of depression is more than $80 billion a year in lost productivity (Scelfo, 2007; Simon et al., 2008; Edoka, Petrou, & Ramchandani, 2011).

Women are twice as likely to experience major depression as men, with one-fourth of all females apt to encounter it at some point during their lives. Furthermore, although no one is sure why, the rate of depression is going up throughout the world. Results of in-depth interviews conducted in the United States, Puerto Rico, Taiwan, Lebanon, Canada, Italy, Germany, and France indicate that the incidence of depression has increased significantly over previous rates in every area. In fact, in some countries, the likelihood that individuals will have major depression at some point in their lives is three times higher than it was for earlier generations. In addition, people are developing major depression at increasingly younger ages (Kendler et al., 2006a; Staley, Sanacora, & Tagman, 2006; Sado et al., 2011).

When psychologists speak of major depression, they do not mean the sadness that comes from experiencing one of life's disappointments that we all have experienced. Some depression is normal after the breakup of a long-term relationship, the death of a loved one, or the loss of a job. It is normal even after less serious problems, such as doing badly on a test or having a romantic partner forget one's birthday.

People who suffer from major depression experience similar feelings, but the severity tends to be considerably greater. They may feel useless, worthless, and lonely, and they may think the future is hopeless and no one can help them. They may lose their appetite and have no energy. Moreover, they may experience such feelings for months or even years. They may cry uncontrollably, have sleep disturbances, and be at risk for suicide. The depth and duration of such behavior are the hallmarks of major depression. (Figure 5 provides a self-assessment of depression.)

Study Alert

Major depression differs from the normal depression that occasionally occurs during most people's lives; major depression is more intense, lasts longer, and may have no clear trigger.

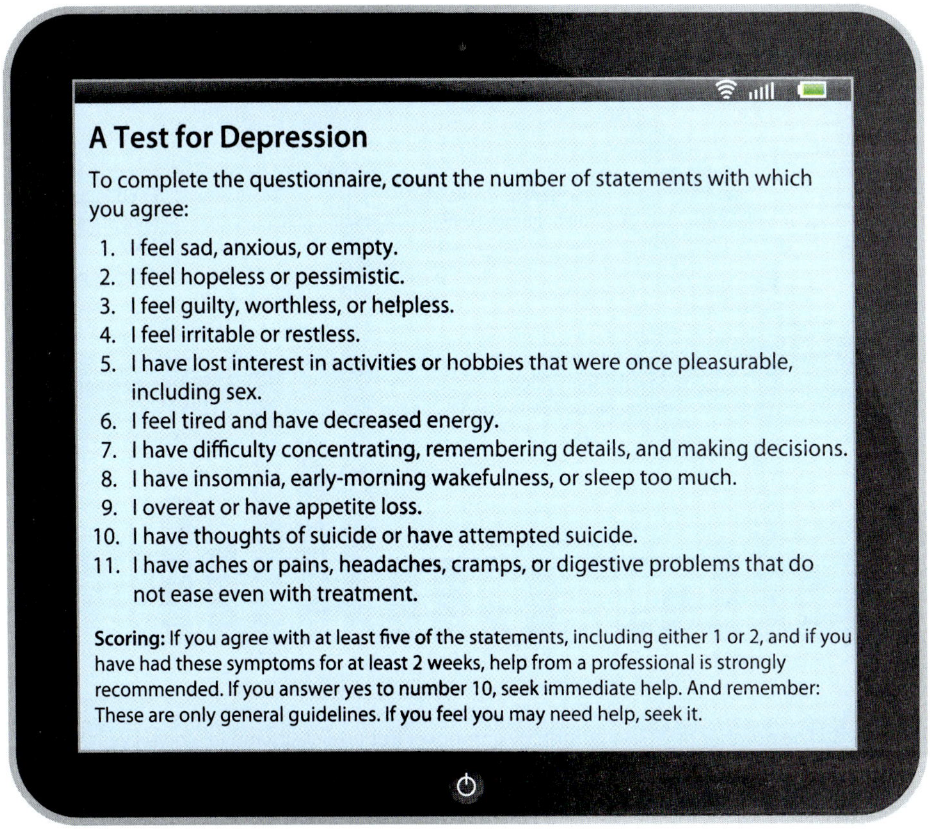

A Test for Depression

To complete the questionnaire, count the number of statements with which you agree:

1. I feel sad, anxious, or empty.
2. I feel hopeless or pessimistic.
3. I feel guilty, worthless, or helpless.
4. I feel irritable or restless.
5. I have lost interest in activities or hobbies that were once pleasurable, including sex.
6. I feel tired and have decreased energy.
7. I have difficulty concentrating, remembering details, and making decisions.
8. I have insomnia, early-morning wakefulness, or sleep too much.
9. I overeat or have appetite loss.
10. I have thoughts of suicide or have attempted suicide.
11. I have aches or pains, headaches, cramps, or digestive problems that do not ease even with treatment.

Scoring: If you agree with at least five of the statements, including either 1 or 2, and if you have had these symptoms for at least 2 weeks, help from a professional is strongly recommended. If you answer yes to number 10, seek immediate help. And remember: These are only general guidelines. If you feel you may need help, seek it.

FIGURE 5 This test is based on the list of signs and symptoms of depression found on the National Institute of Mental Health website at http://www.nimh.nih.gov/health/publications/depression/what-are-the-signs-and-symptoms-of-depression.shtml

MANIA AND BIPOLAR DISORDER

mania An extended state of intense, wild elation.

While depression leads to the depths of despair, mania leads to emotional heights. **Mania** is an extended state of intense, wild elation. People experiencing mania feel intense happiness, power, invulnerability, and energy. Believing they will succeed at anything they attempt, they may become involved in wild schemes. Consider, for example, the following description of an individual who experienced a manic episode:

> Mr. O'Reilly took a leave of absence from his civil service job. He purchased a large number of cuckoo clocks and then an expensive car, which he planned to use as a mobile showroom for his wares, anticipating that he would make a great deal of money. He proceeded to "tear around town" buying and selling clocks and other merchandise, and when he was not out, he was continuously on the phone making "deals." . . . He was $3,000 in debt and had driven his family to exhaustion with his excessive activity and talkativeness. He said, however, that he felt "on top of the world." (Spitzer et al., 1983, p. 115)

bipolar disorder A disorder in which a person alternates between periods of euphoric feelings of mania and periods of depression.

Typically, people sequentially experience periods of mania and depression. This alternation of mania and depression is called **bipolar disorder** (a condition previously known as manic-depressive disorder). The swings between highs and lows may occur a few days apart or may alternate over a period of years. In addition, in bipolar disorder, periods of depression are usually longer than periods of mania.

Ironically, some of society's most creative individuals may have suffered from bipolar disorder. The imagination, drive, excitement, and energy that they display during manic stages allow them to make unusually creative contributions. For instance, historical analysis of the composer Robert Schumann's music shows that he was most prolific during periods of mania. In contrast, his output dropped off drastically during periods of depression (see Figure 6). On the other hand, the high output associated with mania does not necessarily lead to higher quality: Some of Schumann's greatest works were created outside his periods of mania (Ludwig, 1996; Szegedy Maszak, 2003).

Despite the creative fires that may be lit by mania, persons who experience this disorder often show a recklessness that produces emotional and sometimes physical self-injury. They may alienate people with their talkativeness, inflated self-esteem, and indifference to the needs of others.

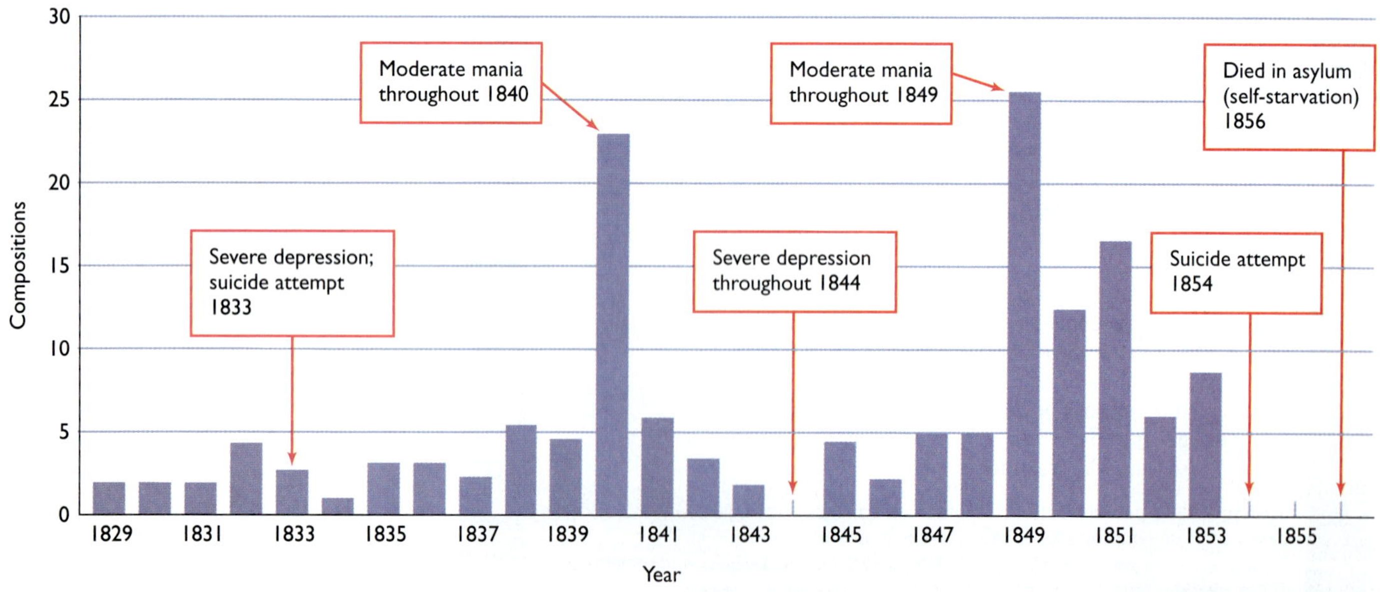

FIGURE 6 The number of pieces written by composer Robert Schumann in a given year is related to his periods of depression and mania (Slater & Meyer, 1959; reprinted in Jamison, 1993). Why do you think mania might be associated with creative productivity in some people?

CAUSES OF MOOD DISORDERS

Because they represent a major mental health problem, mood disorders—and, in particular, depression—have received a good deal of study. Several approaches have been used to explain the disorders.

Some mood disorders clearly have genetic and biochemical roots. In fact, most evidence suggests that bipolar disorders are caused primarily by biological factors. For instance, bipolar disorder (and some forms of major depression) clearly runs in some families, pointing to a genetic cause. Furthermore, researchers have found that several neurotransmitters play a role in depression. For example, alterations in the functioning of serotonin and norepinephrine in the brain are related to the disorder. Finally, research on neuroimaging suggests that a brain structure called area 25 is related to depression: When area 25 is smaller than normal, it is associated with a higher risk of depression (Kato, 2007; Popa et al., 2008; Insel, 2010).

Other explanations for depression have also included a focus on psychological causes. For instance, proponents of psychoanalytic approaches see depression as the result of feelings of loss (real or potential) or of anger directed at oneself. One psychoanalytic approach, for instance, suggests that depression is produced by the loss or threatened loss of a parent early in life (Vanheule et al., 2006).

Behavioral theories of depression argue that the stresses of life produce a reduction in positive reinforcers. As a result, people begin to withdraw, which only reduces positive reinforcers further. In addition, people receive attention for their depressive behavior, which further reinforces the depression (Lewinsohn & Essau, 2002; Lewinsohn et al., 2003).

Some explanations for mood disorders attribute them to cognitive factors. For example, psychologist Martin Seligman suggests that depression is largely a response to learned helplessness. *Learned helplessness* is a learned expectation that events in one's life are uncontrollable and that one cannot escape from the situation. As a consequence, people simply give up fighting aversive events and submit to them, which thereby produces depression. Other theorists go a step further and suggest that depression results from hopelessness, a combination of learned helplessness and an expectation that negative outcomes in one's life are inevitable (Kwon & Laurenceau, 2002; Bjornstad, 2006; Li, B., et al., 2011).

Clinical psychologist Aaron Beck has proposed that faulty cognitions underlie people's depressed feelings. Specifically, his cognitive theory of depression suggests that depressed individuals typically view themselves as life's losers and blame themselves whenever anything goes wrong. By focusing on the negative side of situations, they feel inept and unable to act constructively to change their environment. In sum, their negative cognitions lead to feelings of depression (Newman et al., 2002).

Brain imaging studies suggest that people with depression experience a general blunting of emotional reactions. For example, one study found that the brains of people with depression showed significantly less activation when they viewed photos of human faces displaying strong emotions than did those without the disorder (Gotlib et al., 2004).

Other explanations of depression derive from evolutionary psychology, which considers how our genetic inheritance from our ancestors influences our behavior. In the evolutionary view, depression is an adaptive response to unattainable goals. When people fruitlessly pursue an ever-elusive goal, depression begins, ending pursuit of the goal. Ultimately, when the depression lifts, people can turn to other, more reasonable goals. In this view, depression serves a positive function and in the long run increases the chances of survival for particular individuals, who can then pass the behavior to their offspring. Such reasoning, of course, is highly speculative (Nesse, 2000; Siegert & Ward, 2002; Pfeffer, 2006).

The various theories of depression have not provided a complete answer to an elusive question that has dogged researchers: Why does depression occur in approximately twice as many women as men—a pattern that is similar across a variety of cultures?

One explanation suggests that the stress women experience may be greater than the stress men experience at certain points in their lives—such as when a woman must simultaneously earn a living and be the primary caregiver for her children. In addition, women have a higher risk for physical and sexual abuse, typically earn lower wages than men, report greater unhappiness with their marriages, and generally experience chronic negative circumstances. Furthermore, women and men may respond to stress with different coping mechanisms. For instance, men may abuse drugs, while women respond with depression (Nolen-Hoeksema, 2007; Hyde, Mezulis, & Abramson, 2008; Komarovskaya et al., 2011).

Biological factors may also explain some women's depression. For example, the rate of female depression begins to rise during puberty, so some psychologists believe that hormones make women more vulnerable to the disorder. In addition, 25–50% of women who take oral contraceptives report symptoms of depression, and depression that occurs after the birth of a child is linked to hormonal changes. Finally, structural differences in men's and women's brains that we discussed in the neuroscience and behavior modules may be related to gender differences in depression (Holden, 2005; Graham, Bancroft, & Doll, 2007; Solomon & Herman, 2009).

Ultimately, it is clear that researchers have discovered no definitive solutions to the puzzle of depression, and there are many alternative explanations. Most likely, a complex interaction of several factors causes mood disorders.

Schizophrenia

> Things that relate, the town of Antelope, Oregon, Jonestown, Charlie Manson, the Hillside Strangler, the Zodiac Killer, Watergate, King's trial in L.A., and many more. In the last 7 years alone, over 23 Star Wars scientists committed suicide for no apparent reason. The AIDS cover-up, the conference in South America in 87 had over 1,000 doctors claim that insects can transmit it. To be able to read one's thoughts and place thoughts in one's mind without the person knowing it's being done. Realization is a reality of bioelectromagnetic control, which is thought transfer and emotional control, recording individual brainwave frequencies of thought, sensation, and emotions. (Nolen-Hoeksema, 2007, pp. 385–386)

This excerpt illustrates the efforts of a person with schizophrenia, one of the more severe forms of mental disturbance, to communicate. People with schizophrenia account for by far the largest percentage of those hospitalized for psychological disorders. They are also in many respects the least likely to recover from their difficulties.

schizophrenia A class of disorders in which severe distortion of reality occurs.

Schizophrenia refers to a class of disorders in which severe distortion of reality occurs. Thinking, perception, and emotion may deteriorate; the individual may withdraw from social interaction; and the person may display bizarre behavior. The symptoms displayed by persons with schizophrenia may vary considerably over time. Nonetheless, a number of characteristics reliably distinguish schizophrenia from other disorders. They include the following:

- *Decline from a previous level of functioning*. An individual can no longer carry out activities he or she was once able to do.
- *Disturbances of thought and speech*. People with schizophrenia use logic and language in a peculiar way. Their thinking often does not make sense, and their logic is frequently faulty, which is referred to as a *formal thought disorder*. They also do not follow conventional linguistic rules (Penn et al., 1997). Consider, for example, the following response to the question "Why do you think people believe in God?"

  Uh, let's, I don't know why, let's see, balloon travel. He holds it up for you, the balloon. He don't let you fall out, your little legs sticking down through the clouds. He's down to the smokestack, looking through the smoke trying to get the balloon gassed up you know. Way they're flying on top that way, legs sticking out. I don't know, looking down on the ground, heck, that'd make you so dizzy you just stay and sleep you know, hold down and sleep there. I used to be sleep outdoors, you know, sleep outdoors instead of going home. (Chapman & Chapman, 1973, p. 3)

As this selection illustrates, although the basic grammatical structure may be intact, the substance of thinking characteristic of schizophrenia is often illogical, garbled, and lacking in meaningful content (Holden, 2003; Heinrichs, 2005).

FIGURE 7 This unusual art was created by an individual suffering from severe mental disturbance.

- *Delusions*. People with schizophrenia often have delusions, firmly held, unshakable beliefs with no basis in reality. Among the common delusions people with schizophrenia experience are the beliefs that they are being controlled by someone else, they are being persecuted by others, and their thoughts are being broadcast so that others know what they are thinking (Coltheart, Langdon, & McKay, 2007; Startup, Bucci, & Langdon, 2009).
- *Hallucinations and perceptual disorders*. People with schizophrenia do not perceive the world as most other people do. They also may have *hallucinations,* the experience of perceiving things that do not actually exist. Furthermore, they may see, hear, or smell things differently from others (see Figure 7); they do not even have a sense of their bodies in the way that others do and have difficulty determining where their bodies stop and the rest of the world begins (Botvinick, 2004; Thomas et al., 2007; Bauer et al., 2011).
- *Emotional disturbances*. People with schizophrenia sometimes show a lack of emotion in which even the most dramatic events produce little or no emotional response. Conversely, they may display emotion that is inappropriate to a situation. For example, a person with schizophrenia may laugh uproariously at a funeral or react with anger when being helped by someone.
- *Withdrawal*. People with schizophrenia tend to have little interest in others. They tend not to socialize or hold real conversations with others, although they may talk at another person. In the most extreme cases, they do not even acknowledge the presence of other people and appear to be in their own isolated world.

Usually, the onset of schizophrenia occurs in early adulthood, and the symptoms follow one of two primary courses. In *process schizophrenia,* the symptoms develop slowly and subtly. There may be a gradual withdrawal from the world, excessive daydreaming, and a blunting of emotion until eventually the disorder reaches the point where others cannot overlook it. In other cases, known as *reactive schizophrenia,* the onset of symptoms is sudden and conspicuous. The treatment outlook for reactive schizophrenia is relatively favorable, but process schizophrenia has proved more difficult to treat.

DSM-5 classifies the symptoms of schizophrenia into two types. Positive-symptom schizophrenia is indicated by the presence of disordered behavior such as hallucinations, delusions, and emotional extremes. In contrast, negative-symptom schizophrenia shows an absence or loss of normal functioning, such as social withdrawal or blunted emotions. Schizophrenia researchers sometimes speak of *Type I schizophrenia,* in which positive symptoms are dominant, and *Type II schizophrenia,* in which negative symptoms are more prominent (Buchanan et al., 2007; Levine & Rabinowitz, 2007).

Study Alert

In Type I schizophrenia, positive symptoms (in which hallucinations, delusions, and emotional extremes are present) are dominant; in Type II schizophrenia, negative symptoms (characterized by an absence or loss of normal functioning) are dominant.

The distinction between Type I and Type II schizophrenia is important because it suggests that two different processes might trigger schizophrenia. Furthermore, it has implications for predicting treatment outcomes.

Risk of Developing Schizophrenia, Based on Genetic Relatedness to a Person with Schizophrenia

Relationship	Genetic Relatedness, %	Risk of Developing Schizophrenia, %
Identical twin	100	48
Child of two schizophrenic parents	100	46
Fraternal twin	50	17
Offspring of one schizophrenic parent	50	17
Sibling	50	9
Nephew or niece	25	4
Spouse	0	2
Unrelated person	0	1

FIGURE 8 The closer the genetic links between two people, the greater the likelihood that if one experiences schizophrenia, so will the other sometime during his or her lifetime. However, genetics is not the full story; if it were, the risk of identical twins having schizophrenia would be 100% and not the 48% shown in this figure. (Source: Gottesman, 1991.)

SOLVING THE PUZZLE OF SCHIZOPHRENIA: BIOLOGICAL CAUSES

Although schizophrenic behavior clearly departs radically from normal behavior, its causes are less apparent. It does appear, however, that schizophrenia has both biological and environmental origins (Sawa & Snyder, 2002).

Let's first consider the evidence pointing to a biological cause. Because schizophrenia is more common in some families than in others, genetic factors seem to be involved in producing at least a susceptibility to or readiness for developing schizophrenia. For example, the closer the genetic link between a person with schizophrenia and another individual, the greater the likelihood that the other person will experience the disorder (see Figure 8; Brzustowicz et al., 2000; Plomin & McGuffin, 2003; Gottesman & Hanson, 2005).

However, if genetics alone were responsible for schizophrenia, the chance of both of two identical twins having schizophrenia would be 100% instead of just under 50% because identical twins have the same genetic makeup. Moreover, attempts to find a link between schizophrenia and a particular gene have been only partly successful. Apparently, genetic factors alone do not produce schizophrenia (Franzek & Beckmann, 1996; Lenzenweger & Dworkin, 1998).

One intriguing biological hypothesis to explain schizophrenia is that the brains of people with the disorder may harbor either a biochemical imbalance or a structural abnormality. For example, the *dopamine hypothesis* suggests that schizophrenia occurs when there is excess activity in the areas of the brain that use dopamine as a neurotransmitter. This hypothesis came to light after the discovery that drugs that block dopamine action in brain pathways can be highly effective in reducing the symptoms of schizophrenia. Other research suggests that glutamate, another neurotransmitter, may be a major contributor to the disorder (Stone, Morrison, & Pilowsky, 2007; Howes & Kapur, 2009; Kendler & Schaffner, 2011).

Some biological explanations propose that structural abnormalities exist in the brains of people with schizophrenia perhaps as a result of exposure to a virus during prenatal development. For example, individuals with schizophrenia show abnormalities in the neural circuits of the cortex and limbic systems, as well as differences in brain functioning (see Figure 9 *Neuroscience in Your Life;* Bartzokis et al., 2003; Reichenberg & Harvey, 2007; Reichenberg et al., 2009).

Further evidence for the importance of biological factors shows that when people with schizophrenia hear voices during hallucinations, the parts of the brain responsible for hearing and language processing become active. When they have visual

Neuroscience in Your Life: Brain Changes with Schizophrenia

FIGURE 9 Changes in the brain have been found in people with schizophrenia. In an MRI reconstruction of the brain of a person with schizophrenia (a), the hippocampi (yellow) are shrunken, and the ventricles (gray) are enlarged and fluid-filled. In contrast, an MRI reconstruction of the brain of a person without the disorder (b) is structurally different with larger hippocampi and smaller ventricles. (Source: N.C. Andreasen, University of Iowa.)

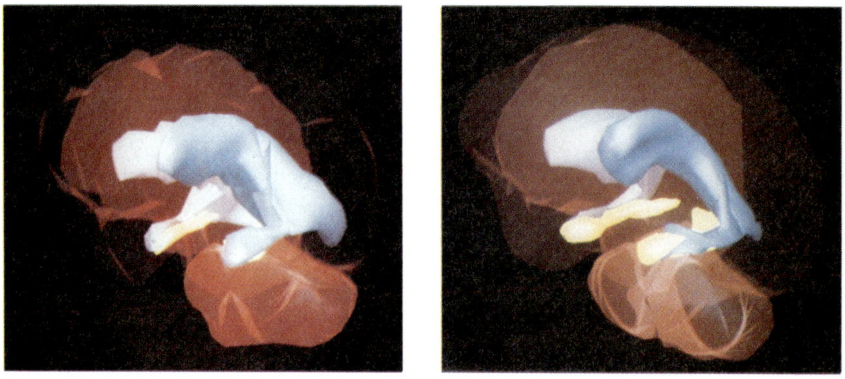

(a) (b)

hallucinations, the parts of the brain involved in movement and color are active. At the same time, people with schizophrenia often have unusually low activity in the brain's frontal lobes—the parts of the brain involved with emotional regulation, insight, and the evaluation of sensory stimuli (Stern & Silbersweig, 2001).

ENVIRONMENTAL PERSPECTIVES ON SCHIZOPHRENIA

Although biological factors provide important pieces of the puzzle of schizophrenia, we still need to consider past and current experiences in the environments of people who develop the disturbance. For instance, psychoanalytic approaches suggest that schizophrenia is a form of regression to earlier experiences and stages of life. Freud believed that people with schizophrenia lack egos that are strong enough to cope with their unacceptable impulses. They regress to the oral stage—a time when the id and ego are not yet separated. Therefore, individuals with schizophrenia essentially lack an ego and act out impulses without concern for reality.

Although this reasoning is theoretically plausible, little evidence supports psychoanalytic explanations. Somewhat more convincing theories look toward the emotional and communication patterns of the families of people with schizophrenia. For instance, some researchers suggest that schizophrenia is related to a family interaction style known as expressed emotion. *Expressed emotion* is an interaction style characterized by high levels of criticism, hostility, and emotional intrusiveness within a family. Other researchers suggest that faulty communication patterns lie at the heart of schizophrenia (Miklowitz & Thompson, 2003; Lobban, Barrowclough, & Jones, 2006).

Psychologists who take a cognitive perspective on schizophrenia suggest that the problems in thinking that people with the disorder experience point to a cognitive cause. Some suggest that schizophrenia results from *overattention* to stimuli in the environment. Rather than being able to screen out unimportant or inconsequential stimuli and focus on the most important things in the environment, people with schizophrenia may be excessively receptive to virtually everything in their environment. As a consequence, their information-processing capabilities become overloaded and eventually break down. Other cognitive experts argue that schizophrenia results from *underattention* to certain stimuli. According to this explanation, people with schizophrenia fail to focus sufficiently on important stimuli and pay attention to other, less important information in their surroundings (Cadenhead & Braff, 1995).

Although it is plausible that overattention and underattention are related to different forms of schizophrenia, these phenomena do not explain the origins of such information-processing disorders. Consequently, cognitive approaches—like other environmental explanations—do not provide a full explanation of the disorder.

THE MULTIPLE CAUSES OF SCHIZOPHRENIA

The major approach now used to explain the onset of schizophrenia involves both biological and situational factors. The *predisposition model of schizophrenia* suggests that individuals may inherit a predisposition or an inborn sensitivity to schizophrenia. This genetic predisposition, then, makes them particularly vulnerable to stressful factors in the environment, such as social rejection or dysfunctional family communication patterns. The stressors may vary, but if they are strong enough and are coupled with a genetic predisposition, they result in the appearance of schizophrenia. Furthermore, a strong genetic predisposition may lead to the onset of schizophrenia even when the environmental stressors are relatively weak.

Study Alert
Remember that the multiple causes of schizophrenia include biological and environmental factors.

In short, the models used today associate schizophrenia with several kinds of biological and environmental factors. It is increasingly clear, then, that no single factor but a combination of interrelated variables produces schizophrenia (Meltzer, 2000; McDonald & Murray, 2004; Opler et al., 2008).

Personality Disorders

> I had always wanted lots of things; as a child I can remember wanting a bullet that a friend of mine had brought in to show the class. I took it and put it into my school bag and when my friend noticed it was missing, I was the one who stayed after school with him and searched the room, and I was the one who sat with him and bitched about the other kids and how one of them took his bullet. I even went home with him to help him break the news to his uncle, who had brought it home from the war for him.
>
> But that was petty compared with the stuff I did later. I wanted a Ph.D. very badly, but I didn't want to work very hard—just enough to get by. I never did the experiments I reported; hell, I was smart enough to make up the results. I knew enough about statistics to make anything look plausible. I got my master's degree without even spending one hour in a laboratory. I mean, the professors believed anything. I'd stay out all night drinking and being with my friends, and the next day I'd get in just before them and tell 'em I'd been in the lab all night. They'd actually feel sorry for me. (Duke & Nowicki, 1979, pp. 309–310)

personality disorder A disorder characterized by a set of inflexible, maladaptive behavior patterns that keep a person from functioning appropriately in society.

This excerpt provides a graphic first-person account of a person with a personality disorder. A **personality disorder** is characterized by a set of inflexible, maladaptive behavior patterns that keep a person from functioning appropriately in society. Personality disorders differ from the other problems we have discussed because those affected by them often have little sense of personal distress associated with the psychological maladjustment. In fact, people with personality disorders frequently lead seemingly normal lives. However, just below the surface lies a set of inflexible, maladaptive personality traits that do not permit these individuals to function as members of society (Davis & Millon, 1999; Clarkin & Lenzenweger, 2004; Friedman, Oltmanns, & Turkheimer, 2007).

The best-known type of personality disorder, illustrated by the case above, is the **antisocial personality disorder** (sometimes referred to as a sociopathic personality). Individuals with this disturbance show no regard for the moral and ethical rules of society or the rights of others. Although they can appear quite intelligent and likable (at least at first), upon closer examination they turn out to be manipulative and deceptive. Moreover, they lack any guilt or anxiety about their wrongdoing. When those with antisocial personality disorder behave in a way that injures someone else, they understand intellectually that they have caused harm but feel no remorse (Goodwin & Hamilton, 2003; Hilarski, 2007; Bateman, 2011).

antisocial personality disorder A disorder in which individuals show no regard for the moral and ethical rules of society or the rights of others.

Study Alert

Unlike most psychological disorders, personality disorders produce little or no personal distress.

People with antisocial personality disorder are often impulsive and lack the ability to withstand frustration. They can be extremely manipulative. They also may have excellent social skills; they can be charming, engaging, and highly persuasive. Some of the best con artists have antisocial personalities.

What causes such an unusual constellation of problem behaviors? A variety of factors have been suggested ranging from an inability to experience emotions appropriately to problems in family relationships. For example, in many cases of antisocial behavior, the individual has come from a home in which a parent has died or left or one in which there is a lack of affection, a lack of consistency in discipline, or outright rejection. Other explanations concentrate on sociocultural factors because an unusually high proportion of people with antisocial personalities come from lower socioeconomic groups. Still, no one has been able to pinpoint the specific causes of antisocial personalities, and it is likely that some combination of factors is responsible (Rosenstein & Horowitz, 1996; Costa & Widiger, 2002; Chen et al., 2011).

People with **borderline personality disorder** have difficulty developing a secure sense of who they are. As a consequence, they tend to rely on relationships with others to define their identity. The problem with this strategy is that rejections are devastating. Furthermore, people with this disorder distrust others and have difficulty controlling their anger. Their emotional volatility leads to impulsive and self-destructive behavior. Individuals with borderline personality disorder often feel empty and alone, and they have difficulty cooperating with others. They may form intense, sudden, one-sided relationships in which they demand the attention of another person and then feel angry when they don't receive it. One reason for this behavior is that they may have a background in which others discounted or criticized their emotional reactions, and they may not have learned to regulate their emotions effectively (Links, Eynan, & Heisel, 2007; King-Casas et al., 2008; Hopwood et al., 2009).

borderline personality disorder A disorder in which individuals have difficulty developing a secure sense of who they are.

Another example of a personality disturbance is the **narcissistic personality disorder,** which is characterized by an exaggerated sense of self-importance. Those with the disorder expect special treatment from others while at the same time disregarding others' feelings. In some ways, in fact, the main attribute of the narcissistic personality is an inability to experience empathy for other people.

narcissistic personality disorder A personality disturbance characterized by an exaggerated sense of self-importance.

There are several other categories of personality disorder that range in severity from individuals who may simply be regarded by others as eccentric, obnoxious, or difficult to people who act in a manner that is criminal and dangerous to others. Although they are not out of touch with reality like people with schizophrenia, people with personality disorders lead lives that put them on the fringes of society (Millon, Davis, & Millon, 2000; Trull & Widiger, 2003).

Childhood Disorders

We typically view childhood as a time of innocence and relative freedom from stress. In reality, though, almost 20% of children and 40% of adolescents experience significant emotional or behavioral disorders (Romano et al., 2001; Broidy, Nagin, & Tremblay, 2003; Nolen-Hoeksema, 2007).

For example, although major depression is more prevalent in adults, around 2.5% of children and more than 8% of adolescents suffer from the disorder. In fact, by the time they reach age 20, between 15% and 20% of children and adolescents will experience an episode of major depression (Garber & Horowitz, 2002).

Children do not always display depression the same way adults do. Rather than showing profound sadness or hopelessness, childhood depression may produce the expression of exaggerated fears, clinginess, or avoidance of everyday activities. In older children, the symptoms may be sulking, school problems, and even acts of delinquency (Wenar, 1994; Koplewicz, 2002; Seroczynski, Jacquez, & Cole, 2003).

attention-deficit hyperactivity disorder (ADHD) A disorder marked by inattention, impulsiveness, a low tolerance for frustration, and a great deal of inappropriate activity.

A considerably more common childhood disorder is **attention-deficit hyperactivity disorder,** or **ADHD,** a disorder marked by inattention, impulsiveness, a low tolerance for frustration, and generally a great deal of inappropriate activity. Although all children show such behavior some of the time, it is so common in children diagnosed with ADHD that it interferes with their everyday functioning (Barkley, 2005; Smith, Barkley, & Shapiro, 2006; Barkley, Knouse, & Murphy, 2011).

ADHD is surprisingly widespread with estimates ranging between 3% and 5% of the school-age population—or some 3.5 million children under the age of 18 in the United States. Children diagnosed with the disorder are often exhausting to parents and teachers, and even their peers find them difficult to deal with.

The cause of ADHD is not known, although most experts feel that it is produced by dysfunctions in the nervous system. For example, one theory suggests that unusually low levels of arousal in the central nervous system cause ADHD. To compensate, children with ADHD seek out stimulation to increase arousal. Still, such theories are speculative. Furthermore, because many children occasionally show behaviors characteristic of ADHD, it often is misdiagnosed or in some cases overdiagnosed. Only the frequency and persistence of the symptoms of ADHD allow for a correct diagnosis, which only a trained professional can do (Barkley, 2000; Sciutto & Eisenberg, 2007).

autism spectrum disorder A severe developmental disability that impairs children's ability to communicate and relate to others.

Autism spectrum disorder, a severe developmental disability that impairs one's ability to communicate and relate to others, is another disorder that usually appears in the first 3 years and typically continues throughout life. Children with autism have difficulties in both verbal and nonverbal communication, and they may avoid social contact. About one in 88 children are now thought to have the disorder, and its prevalence has risen significantly in the last decade. Whether the increase is the result of an actual rise in the incidence of autism or is due to better reporting is a question of intense debate among researchers (Rice, 2009).

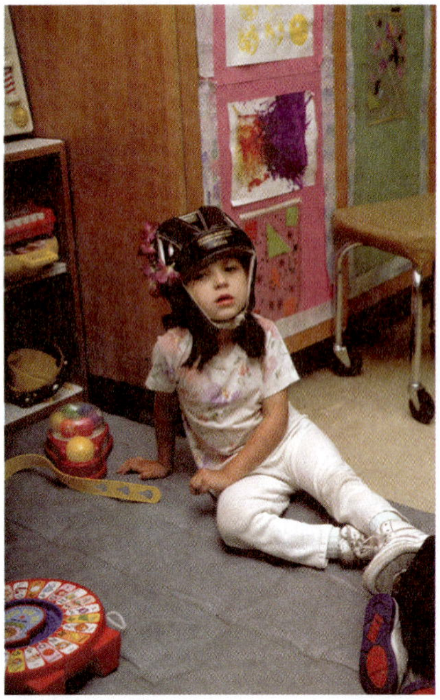

In the most severe cases of autism spectrum disorder, children display self-injurious behavior and must wear protective head gear.

Other Disorders

It's important to keep in mind that the various forms of psychological disorders described in *DSM-5* cover much more ground than we have been able to discuss in this module. Some relate to topics previously considered in other chapters. For example, *psychoactive substance use disorder* relates to problems that arise from the use and abuse of drugs. Furthermore, *alcohol use disorders* are among the most serious and widespread problems. Both psychoactive substance use disorder and alcohol use disorder co-occur with many other psychological disorders such as mood disorders, posttraumatic stress disorder, and schizophrenia, which complicates treatment considerably (Salgado, Quinlan, & Zlotnick, 2007).

Another widespread problem is *eating disorders.* They include such disorders as *anorexia nervosa* and *bulimia,* which we considered in the chapter on motivation and emotion, as well as *binge-eating disorder,* characterized by binge eating without behaviors designed to prevent weight gain. Finally, *sexual disorders,* in which one's sexual activity is unsatisfactory, are another important class of problems. They include *sexual desire disorders, sexual arousal disorders,* and *paraphilic disorders,* atypical sexual activities that may include nonhuman objects or nonconsenting partners.

Another important class of disorders is *organic mental disorders,* some of which we touched on previously. These are problems that have a purely biological basis, such as Alzheimer's disease and some types of mental retardation. Remember, there are other disorders that we have not mentioned at all, and each of the classes we have discussed can be divided into several subcategories (Kopelman & Fleminger, 2002; Pratt et al., 2003; Reijonen et al., 2003).

RECAP/EVALUATE/RETHINK

RECAP

LO 38-1 What are the major psychological disorders?

- Anxiety disorders are present when a person experiences so much anxiety that it affects daily functioning. Specific types of anxiety disorders include phobic disorder, panic disorder, and generalized anxiety disorder. Also related is obsessive-compulsive disorder. (pp. 463, 464)
- Somatoform disorders are psychological difficulties that take on a physical (somatic) form but for which there is no medical cause. Examples are hypochondriasis and conversion disorders. (p. 468)
- Dissociative disorders are marked by the separation, or dissociation, of different facets of a person's personality that are usually integrated. Major kinds of dissociative disorders include dissociative identity disorder, dissociative amnesia, and dissociative fugue. (pp. 468, 469)
- Mood disorders are characterized by emotional states of depression or euphoria so strong that they intrude on everyday living. They include major depression and bipolar disorder. (pp. 470–472)
- Schizophrenia is one of the more severe forms of mental illness. Symptoms of schizophrenia include declines in functioning, thought and language disturbances, perceptual disorders, emotional disturbance, and withdrawal from others. (p. 474)
- Strong evidence links schizophrenia to genetic, biochemical, and environmental factors. According to the predisposition model, an interaction among various factors produces the disorder. (pp. 476–478)
- People with personality disorders experience little or no personal distress, but they do suffer from an inability to function as normal members of society. These disorders include antisocial personality disorder, borderline personality disorder, and narcissistic personality disorder. (pp. 478, 479)
- Childhood disorders include major depression, attention-deficit hyperactivity disorder (ADHD), and autism spectrum disorder. (p. 479, 480)

EVALUATE

1. Kathy is terrified of elevators. She could be suffering from a(n)
   a. Obsessive-compulsive disorder
   b. Phobic disorder
   c. Panic disorder
   d. Generalized anxiety disorder
2. Carmen described an incident in which her anxiety suddenly rose to a peak, and she felt a sense of impending doom. Carmen experienced a(n) __________ __________.
3. Troubling thoughts that persist for weeks or months are known as
   a. Obsessions
   b. Compulsions
   c. Rituals
   d. Panic attacks
4. An overpowering urge to carry out a strange ritual is called a(n) __________.
5. The separation of the personality, which provides escape from stressful situations, is the key factor in __________ disorders.
6. States of extreme euphoria and energy paired with severe depression characterize __________ disorder.
7. __________ schizophrenia is characterized by symptoms that are sudden and of easily identifiable onset; __________ schizophrenia develops gradually over a person's life span.
8. The __________ __________ states that schizophrenia may be caused by an excess of certain neurotransmitters in the brain.

RETHINK

1. What cultural factors might contribute to the rate of anxiety disorders found in a culture? How might the experience of anxiety differ among people of different cultures?
2. *From the perspective of a social worker:* Personality disorders are often not apparent to others, and many people with these problems seem to live basically normal lives and are not a threat to others. Because these people often appear from the outside to function well in society, why should they be considered psychologically disordered?

Answers to Evaluate Questions

1. b; 2. panic attack; 3. a; 4. compulsion; 5. dissociative; 6. bipolar; 7. Reactive, process; 8. dopamine hypothesis

KEY TERMS

anxiety disorder p. 463
phobias p. 464
panic disorder p. 464
generalized anxiety disorder p. 465
obsessive-compulsive disorder (OCD) p. 465
obsession p. 465
compulsion p. 465
somatoform disorders p. 468
hypochondriasis p. 468
conversion disorder p. 468
dissociative disorders p. 468
dissociative identity disorder (DID) p. 469
dissociative amnesia p. 469
dissociative fugue p. 470
mood disorder p. 470
major depression p. 470
mania p. 472
bipolar disorder p. 472
schizophrenia p. 474
personality disorder p. 478
antisocial personality disorder p. 479
borderline personality disorder p. 479
narcissistic personality disorder p. 479
attention-deficit hyperactivity disorder (ADHD) p. 480
autism spectrum disorder p. 480

MODULE 39

Psychological Disorders in Perspective

How common are the kinds of psychological disorders we've been discussing? Here's one answer: Every second person you meet in the United States is likely to suffer at some point during his or her life from a psychological disorder.

That's the conclusion drawn from a massive study on the prevalence of psychological disorders. In that study, researchers conducted face-to-face interviews with more than 8,000 men and women between the ages of 15 and 54. The sample was designed to be representative of the population of the United States. According to results of the study, 48% of those interviewed had experienced a disorder at some point in their lives. In addition, 30% experienced a disorder in any particular year. Furthermore, a significant number of people experienced simultaneous multiple disorders—a situation known as *comorbidity* (Welkowitz et al., 2000; Merikangas et al., 2007; Kessler & Wang, 2008).

The most common disorder reported in the study was depression; 17% of those surveyed reported at least one major episode. Ten percent had suffered from depression during the current year. The next most common disorder was alcohol dependence, which occurred at a lifetime incidence rate of 14%. In addition, 7% of those interviewed had experienced alcohol dependence in the last year. Other frequently occurring psychological disorders were drug dependence, disorders involving panic (such as an overwhelming fear of talking to strangers and terror of heights), and posttraumatic stress disorder.

Although some researchers think the estimates of severe disorders may be too high (Narrow et al., 2002), the national findings are consistent with studies of college students and their psychological difficulties. For example, in one study of the problems of students who visited a college counseling center, more than 40% of students reported being depressed (see Figure 1 on page 484). These figures include only students who sought help from the counseling center and not those who did not seek treatment. Consequently, the figures are not representative of the entire college population (Benton et al., 2003; also see *Applying Psychology in the 21st Century* on page 486).

The significant level of psychological disorders is a problem not only in the United States; according to the World Health Organization, mental health difficulties are also a global concern. Throughout the world, psychological disorders are widespread. Furthermore, there are economic disparities in treatment; more affluent people with mild disorders receive more and better treatment than poor people who have more severe disorders. In fact, psychological disorders make up 14% of global illness, and 90% of people in developing countries receive no care at all for their disorders (see Figure 2 on page 485; WHO World Mental Health Survey Consortium, 2004; Jacob et al., 2007; Wang et al., 2007).

Also, keep in mind that the incidence of specific disorders varies significantly in other cultures. For instance, cross-cultural surveys show that the incidence of major depression varies significantly from one culture to another. The probability of having at least one episode of depression is only 1.5% in Taiwan and 2.9% in Korea compared with 11.6% in New Zealand and 16.4% in France. Such notable differences underscore the importance of considering the cultural context of psychological disorders (Weissman et al., 1997; Tseng, 2003).

Learning Outcomes

LO 39-1 How prevalent are psychological disorders?

LO 39-2 What indicators signal a need for the help of a mental health practitioner?

Study Alert

Remember that the incidence of various types of psychological disorders in the general population is surprisingly high.

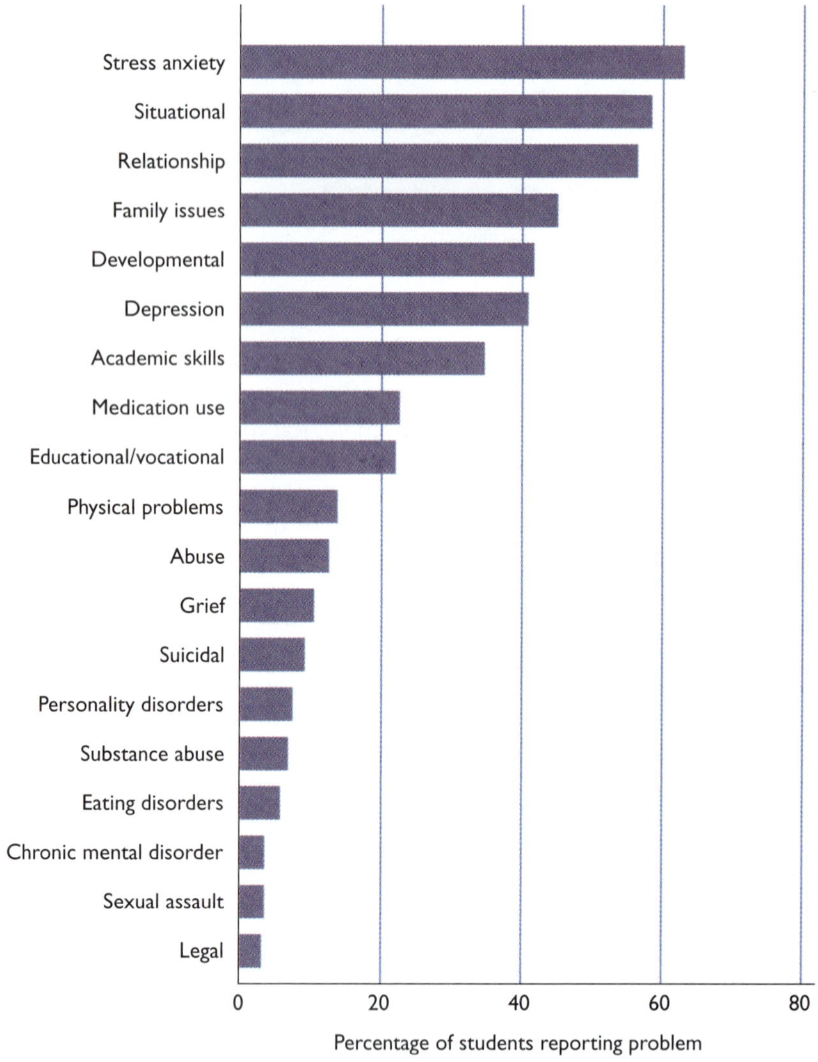

FIGURE 1 The problems reported by students visiting a college counseling center. Would you have predicted this pattern of psychological difficulties? (Source: Benton et al., 2003.)

The Social and Cultural Context of Psychological Disorders

In considering the nature of the psychological disorders described in *DSM-5,* it's important to keep in mind that the disorders that were included in the manual are a reflection of Western culture at the start of the 21st century. The classification system provides a snapshot of how its authors viewed mental disorder when it was published. In fact, the development of the most recent version of the *DSM* was a source of great debate, which in part reflects issues that divide society.

One specific newly classified disorder that has been added to DSM-5 has caused controversy is known as *disruptive mood dysregulation disorder.* This particular diagnosis is characterized by temperamental outbursts grossly out of proportion to the situation, both verbally and physically, in children between the ages of 6 and 18. Some practitioners argue these symptoms simply define a child having a temper tantrum rather than a disorder (Dobbs, 2012; Marchand & Phillips McEnany, 2012; Frances, 2013).

Study Alert

It is important to understand that the *DSM* is a living document that presents a view of disorders that reflects the culture and historical context of its authors.

Similarly, someone who overeats 12 times in three months can be considered to be suffering from the new classification of *binge eating disorder,* which seems to some critics to be overly inclusive. Finally, *hoarding behavior* is now placed in its own

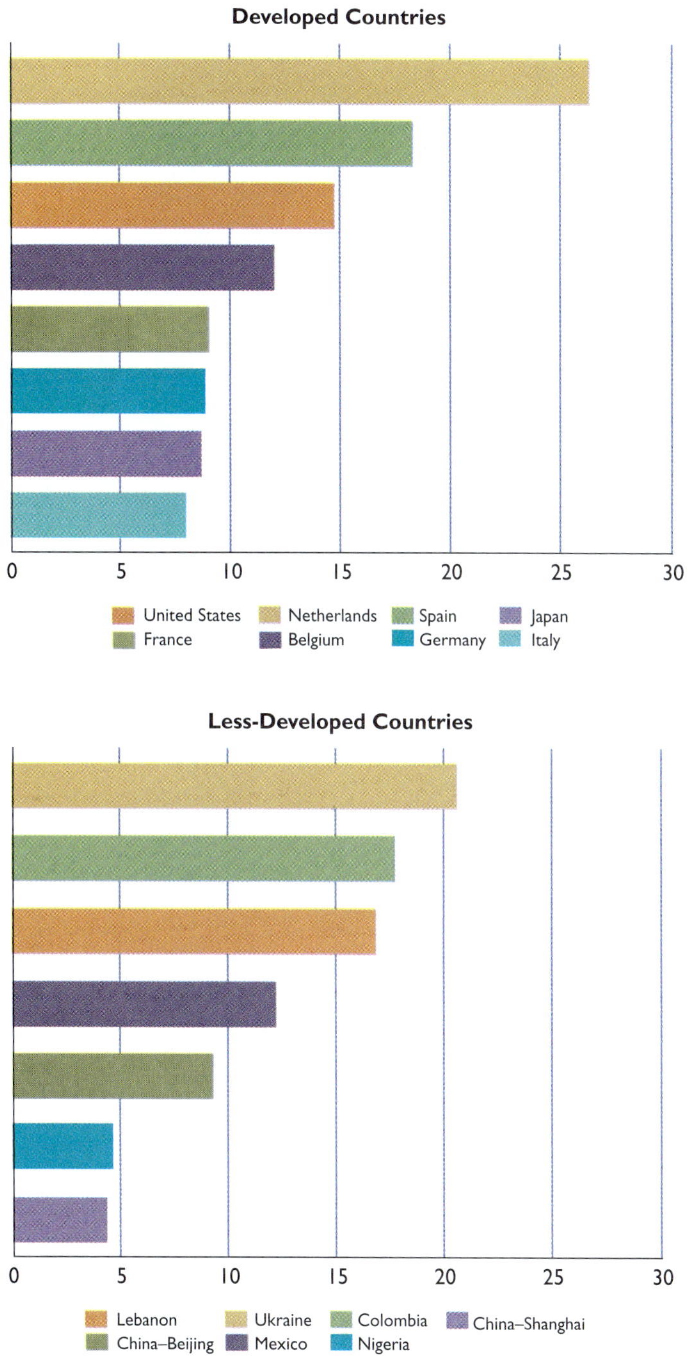

FIGURE 2 According to a global survey conducted by the World Health Organization, the prevalence of psychological disorders is widespread. These figures show the percentage of people who have experienced any psychological disorder within the prior 12-month period. (Source: WHO World Mental Health Survey Consortium, 2004, Table 3.)

category of psychological disorder. Some critics suggest this change is more a reflection of the rise of reality shows focusing on hoarding rather than reflecting a distinct category of psychological disturbance (Hudson et al., 2012).

Such controversies underline the fact that our understanding of abnormal behavior reflects the society and culture in which we live. Future revisions of *DSM* may include a different catalog of disorders. Even now, other cultures might include a list of disorders that are very different from the list that appears in the current *DSM*, as we discuss next.

Applying Psychology in the 21st Century

Psychological Problems Are Increasing Among College Students

Psychological disorders are surprisingly common among college students.

Does the stress of being in college have you feeling anxious or blue? If so, you're far from alone. New research shows that mental health problems, particularly anxiety, are plaguing more college students today than in the past.

One study examined the responses of many thousands of young people on the Minnesota Multiphasic Personality Inventory (MMPI) between 1938 and 2007 and found that indications of mental health problems increased steadily over those 70 years, with 85% of recent college students scoring higher than the average college student in the 1930s and 1940s on measures of psychological problems. The findings showed elevated levels on a number of MMPI scales, including those measuring indicators of paranoia, schizophrenia, mania, and depression (Twenge et al., 2010).

The researchers noted that the increase in mental disorders coincides with increasing emphasis being placed on extrinsic goals such as attaining wealth and status and decreasing emphasis being placed on intrinsic goals such as creating satisfying interpersonal relationships and a sense of community. They speculated that such emphasis on extrinsic goals might encourage unreasonable expectations for personal achievement, causing two problems: undue stress as people try to achieve unattainable goals and a sense of unfulfillment when they fail to live up to their expectations (Eckersley & Dear, 2002; Jacobs, 2010).

Another comprehensive survey of directors of over 400 college and university counseling centers also showed evidence of this increase in psychological problems among college students. Over three-quarters of respondents reported that the number of students with severe psychological problems seen by their staff had increased in the past year. As in past surveys, anxiety and depression were the top two student complaints—but anxiety surpassed depression for the first time since the surveys began in 2006 (Barr et al., 2010).

According to one researcher, Jean Twenge, the findings are a wake-up call. "Students have always had higher anxiety than the general adult population, but the increase over time is startling," she said. "Anxiety is usually a precursor to more serious mental health issues like depression, so it's important to teach young people how to manage their stress now so it doesn't become worse" (Jacobs, 2010).

RETHINK

- What might be some ways that we can teach college students to manage their stress?
- Why might people be putting more emphasis on material goals and less on social ones, even to the detriment of their own psychological health?

Exploring DIVERSITY

DSM and Culture—and the Culture of *DSM*

In most people's estimation, a person who hears voices of the recently deceased is probably a victim of a psychological disturbance. Yet some Plains Indians routinely hear the voices of the dead calling to them from the afterlife.

This is only one example of the role of culture in labeling behavior as "abnormal." In fact, among all the major adult disorders included in the *DSM* categorization, a minority are found across all cultures of the world. Most others are prevalent primarily in North America and Western Europe (Kleinman, 1996; Cohen, Slomkowski, & Robins, 1999; López & Guarnaccia, 2000).

For instance, take anorexia nervosa, the disorder in which people become obsessed with their weight and sometimes stop eating, ultimately starving to death in the process. This disorder occurs most frequently in cultures that hold the societal standard that slender female bodies are the most desirable. In most of the world, where such a standard does not exist, anorexia nervosa is rare. Furthermore, the disorder may appear in specific ways in a particular culture. For instance, in Hong Kong, symptoms of one form of anorexia relate to complaints of bloated stomachs, rather than fears of becoming fat (Watters, 2010).

Similarly, dissociative identity (multiple personality) disorder makes sense as a problem only in societies in which a sense of self is fairly concrete. In India, the self is based more on external factors that are relatively independent of the person. There, when an individual displays symptoms of what people in a Western society would call dissociative identity disorder, Indians assume that that person is possessed either by demons (which they view as a malady) or by gods (which does not require treatment).

Furthermore, even though disorders such as schizophrenia are found throughout the world, cultural factors influence the specific symptoms of the disorder. Hence, catatonic schizophrenia in which unmoving patients appear to be frozen in the same position (sometimes for days), is rare in North America and Western Europe. In contrast, in India, 80% of those with schizophrenia are catatonic.

Other cultures have disorders that do not appear in the West. For example, in Malaysia, a behavior called *amok* is characterized by a wild outburst in which a usually quiet and withdrawn person kills or severely injures another. *Koro* is a condition found in Southeast Asian males who develop an intense panic that the penis is about to withdraw into the abdomen. Some West African men develop a disorder when they first attend college that they call "brain fag"; it includes feelings of heaviness or heat in the head as well as depression and anxiety. Finally, *ataque de nervios* is a disorder found most often among Latinos from the Caribbean. It is characterized by trembling, crying, uncontrollable screams, and incidents of verbal or physical aggression (Cohen et al., 1999; López & Guarnaccia, 2000; Adams & Dzokoto, 2007).

Explanations for psychological disorders also differ among cultures. For example, in China, psychological disorders are commonly viewed as a weakness of the heart, a concept that derives from thousands of years of traditional Chinese medicine. Many terms used to describe emotions and symptoms of psychological disorders make direct reference to the heart—but the association isn't simply a metaphorical one. Chinese people are more likely than people in Western cultures to express their emotional anguish in terms of physical symptoms such as heart pain, "heart panic," or "heart vexed." They may also see their emotional pain as merely a side effect of some underlying physical cause or even focus more on the effects that their symptoms are having on their relationships with friends and family members (Miller, 2006; Lee, Kleinman, & Kleinman, 2007; Watters, 2010).

In sum, we should not assume that the *DSM* provides the final word on psychological disorders. The disorders it includes are very much a creation and function of Western cultures at a particular moment in time, and its categories should not be seen as universally applicable (Tseng, 2003).

BECOMING AN INFORMED CONSUMER of Psychology

Deciding When You Need Help

After you've considered the range and variety of psychological disturbances that can afflict people, you may begin to feel that you suffer from one (or more) of the problems we have discussed. In fact, this perception has a name: *medical student's disease*. Although in this case it might more aptly be labeled "psychology student's disease," the basic symptoms are the same: feeling that you suffer from the same sorts of problems you are studying.

Most often, of course, your concerns will be unwarranted. As we have discussed, the differences between normal and abnormal behavior are often so fuzzy that it is easy to jump to the conclusion that you might have the same symptoms that are involved in serious forms of mental disturbance.

Before coming to such a conclusion, though, keep in mind that from time to time we all experience a wide range of emotions, and it is not unusual to feel deeply unhappy, fantasize about bizarre situations, or feel anxiety about life's circumstances. It is the persistence, depth, and consistency of such behavior that set normal reactions apart from abnormal ones. If you have not previously had serious doubts about the normality of your behavior, it is unlikely that reading about others' psychological disorders will prompt you to re-evaluate your earlier conclusion.

On the other hand, many people do have problems that merit concern, and in such cases, it is important to consider the possibility that professional help is warranted. The following list of symptoms can serve as a guideline to help you determine whether outside intervention might be useful (Engler & Goleman, 1992):

- Long-term feelings of distress that interfere with your sense of well-being, competence, and ability to function effectively in daily activities
- Occasions in which you experience overwhelmingly high stress accompanied by feelings of inability to cope with the situation
- Prolonged depression or feelings of hopelessness, especially when they do not have any clear cause (such as the death of someone close)
- Withdrawal from other people
- Thoughts of inflicting harm on oneself or suicide
- A chronic physical problem for which no physical cause can be determined
- A fear or phobia that prevents you from engaging in everyday activities
- Feelings that other people are out to get you or are talking about and plotting against you
- Inability to interact effectively with others, preventing the development of friendships and loving relationships

This list offers a rough set of guidelines for determining when the normal problems of everyday living have escalated beyond your ability to deal with them by yourself. In such situations, the *least* reasonable approach would be to pore over the psychological disorders we have discussed in an attempt at self-diagnosis. A more reasonable strategy is to consider seeking professional help.

RECAP/EVALUATE/RETHINK

RECAP

LO 39-1 How prevalent are psychological disorders?

- About half the people in the United States are likely to experience a psychological disorder at some point in their lives; 30% experience a disorder in any specific year. (p. 483)

LO 39-2 What indicators signal a need for the help of a mental health practitioner?

- The signals that indicate a need for professional help include long-term feelings of psychological distress, feelings of inability to cope with stress, withdrawal from other people, thoughts of inflicting harm on oneself or suicide, prolonged feelings of hopelessness, chronic physical problems with no apparent causes, phobias and compulsions, paranoia, and an inability to interact with others. (p. 488)

EVALUATE

1. The latest version of *DSM* is considered to be the definitive guide to defining psychological disorders. True or false?
2. Match the disorder with the culture in which it is most common:

1. amok	a. India
2. anorexia nervosa	b. Malaysia
3. brain fag	c. United States
4. catatonic schizophrenia	d. West Africa

RETHINK

1. Why is inclusion in the *DSM-5* of disorders such as hoarding behavior so controversial and political? What disadvantages does inclusion bring? Does inclusion bring any benefits?
2. *From the perspective of a college counselor:* What indicators might be most important in determining whether a college student is experiencing a psychological disorder? Do you believe that all students who show signs of a psychological disorder should seek professional help? How might your responses change if the student were from a different culture (e.g., an African society)?

Answers to Evaluate Questions

1. false; the development of the latest version of *DSM* was a source of great controversy, in part reflecting issues that divide society; 2. 1-b, 2-c, 3-d, 4-a

Looking Back

Epilogue

We've discussed some of the many types of psychological disorders to which people are prone, noted the difficulty psychologists and physicians have in clearly differentiating normal from abnormal behavior, and looked at some of the approaches mental health professionals have taken to explain and treat psychological disorders. We considered today's most commonly used classification scheme, categorized in the *DSM-5*, and examined some of the more prevalent forms of psychological disorders. To gain a perspective on the topic of psychological disorders, we discussed the surprisingly broad incidence of psychological disorders in U.S. society and the cultural nature of such disorders.

Turn back to the prologue that described the case of Chris Coles. Using the knowledge you've gained about psychological disorders, consider the following questions.

1. Coles was diagnosed as suffering from schizophrenia. What elements of his behavior seem to fit the description of this disorder?
2. How might each of the perspectives on psychological disorders address the causes of his symptoms?
3. Which perspective provides the most useful explanation for Cole's case, in your opinion, and why?
4. What advantages might there be in using multiple perspectives to address Cole's case?

VISUAL SUMMARY 12 Psychological Disorders

MODULE 37 Normal Versus Abnormal: Making the Distinction

Defining Abnormality

- Deviation from the average
- Deviation from the ideal
- Sense of personal discomfort
- Inability to function effectively
- Legal concept

Perspectives on Abnormality

Perspectives on Psychological Disorders

Perspective	Description	Possible Application of Perspective to Chris's Case
Medical	Assumes that physiological causes are at the root of psychological disorders	Examine Chris for medical problems, such as brain tumor, chemical imbalance in the brain, or disease
Psychoanalytic	Argues that psychological disorders stem from childhood conflicts	Seek out information about Chris's past, considering possible childhood conflicts
Behavioral	Assumes that abnormal behaviors are learned responses	Concentrate on rewards and punishments for Chris's behavior, and identify environmental stimuli that reinforce his behavior
Cognitive	Assumes that cognitions (people's thoughts and beliefs) are central to psychological disorders	Focus on Chris's perceptions of self and his environment
Humanistic	Emphasizes people's responsibility for their own behavior and the need to self-actualize	Consider Chris's behavior in terms of his choices and efforts to reach his potential
Sociocultural	Assumes that behavior is shaped by family, society, and culture	Focus on how societal demands contributed to Chris's disorder

Classifying Abnormal Behavior: *DSM-5* attempts to provide comprehensive and relatively precise definitions for more than 200 disorders.

MODULE 38 Major Psychological Disorders

Anxiety Disorders: Anxiety without external justification

- Phobic disorder
- Panic disorder
- Generalized anxiety disorder
- Causes of anxiety disorders

Obsessive-compulsive Disorder

Somatoform Disorders: Psychological difficulties that take on a physical form with no medical cause

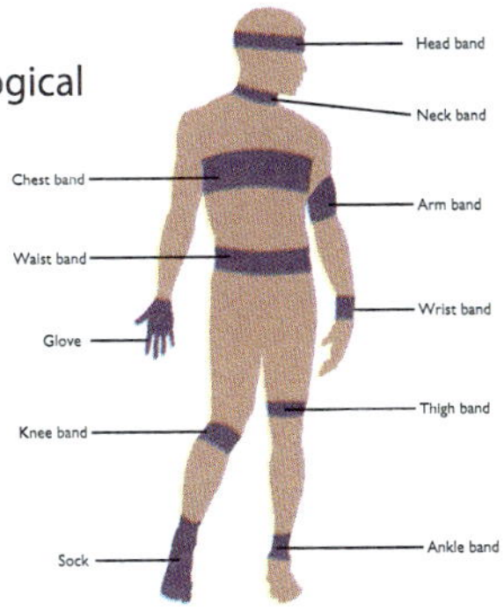

Dissociative Disorders: Separation of different facets of a person's personality that normally work together

Mood Disorders: Disturbances in emotional experience

- Major depression
- Mania and bipolar disorder
- Causes of mood disorders
  - Genetics
  - Psychological: feelings of loss or anger
  - Behavioral: stress
  - Cognitive: learned helplessness and no hope

Schizophrenia: A class of disorders in which distortion of reality occurs

- Decline from a previous level of functioning
- Disturbances of thought and language
- Delusions
- Hallucinations and perceptual disorders
- Emotional disturbances

Personality Disorders: A set of inflexible, maladaptive behavior patterns

- Antisocial personality disorder
- Borderline personality disorder
- Narcissistic personality disorder

Childhood Disorders: Start during childhood or adolescence

- Attention-deficit hyperactivity disorder
- Autism spectrum disorder

MODULE 39 Psychological Disorders in Perspective

Social and Cultural Context: Our understanding of abnormal behavior reflects the society and culture in which we live

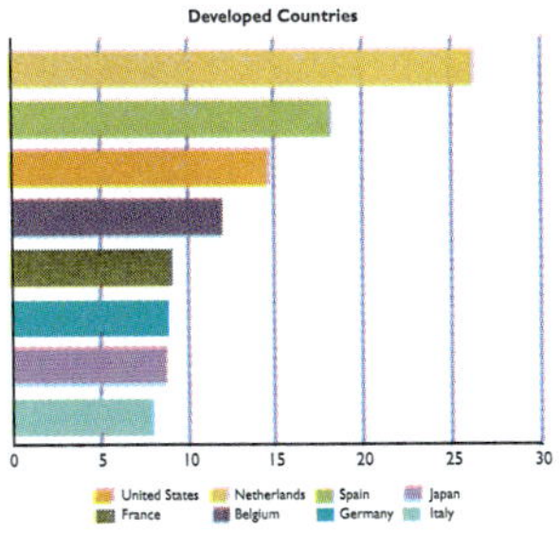

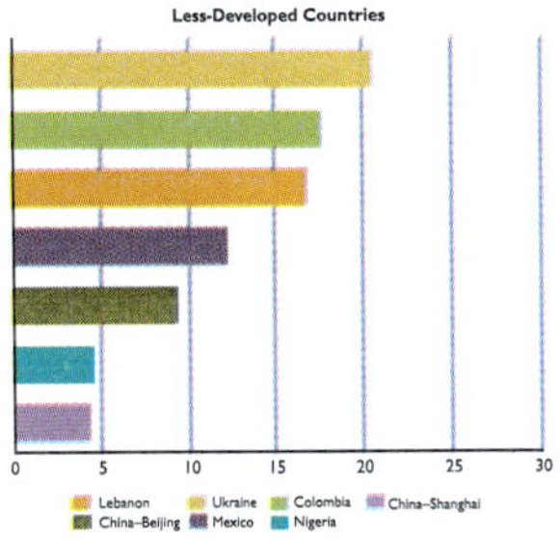